Workbook and Portfolio

For the textbook:

Career Choices

A Guide for Teens and Young Adults:
Who Am I?
What Do I Want?
How Do I Get It?

by Mindy Bingham and Sandy Stryker
Edited by Tanja Easson

Illustrated by Itoko Maeno, Janice Blair, and Diana Lackner

Academic Innovations

This book belongs to _____

Started on _____

Completed on _____

I dedicate this work to _____

 Published by Academic Innovations
(800) 967-8016   FAX (800) 967-4027
www.academicinnovations.com   careerchoices@academicinnovations.com

CONTENTS

My 10-Year Plan and Portfolio   1

How to Use this Workbook   2

Exercises
Section One: Who Am I?

Chapter one   Envisioning Your Future   4
                   How do you define success?

Chapter two   Your Personal Profile   10
                   Getting what you want starts with knowing
                   who you are.

Section Two: What Do I Want?

Chapter three   Lifestyles of the Satisfied and Happy   25
                   Keeping your balance and perspective

Chapter four   What Cost This Lifestyle?   31
                   Every career choice involves sacrifices and rewards

Chapter five   Your Ideal Career   56
                   There's more to consider than just the work

Chapter six   Career Research   66
                   Reading about careers isn't enough

Chapter seven   Decision Making   79
                   How to choose what's best for you

Section Three: How Do I Get It?

Chapter eight   Setting Goals and Solving Problems   85
                   Skills for successful living

Chapter nine   Avoiding Detours and Roadblocks   88
                   The road to success is dotted with many
                   tempting parking places

Chapter ten   Attitude Is Everything   103
                   Learning to accentuate the positive

Chapter eleven   Getting Experience   110
                   Finding your first job

Chapter twelve   Where Do You Go from Here?   115
                   Writing your 10-year plan

My Career Portfolio Notebook   126

My10yearPlan.com   128

Checkpoints   132

Know thyself

This is one of the most challenging, yet important, tasks of our lives. People who know who they are and what they want have a better chance of achieving their own form of success and, ultimately, finding happiness and personal satisfaction. Your workbook will be a record of this exciting adventure and important time in your life.

My 10-Year Plan and Portfolio

The cornerstone of your *Career Choices* experience is the development of a 10-year education, career, and life plan. All the work you do throughout your workbook comes together to form this comprehensive plan.

By the end of your course, after you've read your *Career Choices* textbook and completed all the activities in your workbook, you'll have the tools and data to create either:

- a hard copy portfolio notebook or
- an online version of your 10-year plan and portfolio using the *optional* My10yearplan.com

You will want to be sure to update your 10-year plan and portfolio and use it throughout your life. This valuable document will be a handy resource when you:

- Go to job interviews
- Participate in college interviews
- Meet with your counselors or advisors
- Want to re-evaluate your life choices

Think of this *Workbook and Portfolio* as you would a journal. It will be a lasting record of this transformational time of your life. You'll want to take it home and keep it with your albums, journals, and diaries. Who knows, someday you may want to share it with a special young person in your life.

How to Use this Workbook

All the exercises in *Career Choices,* along with directions, are reprinted in this workbook. To make the most of this workbook, follow this simple process.

STEP ONE:

Read your assignment in the main *Career Choices* textbook and participate in your classroom discussion.

STEP TWO:

Complete the associated written activity. You'll find that particular exercise by opening your workbook and locating the corresponding *Career Choices* textbook page number found in the boxes in the margin that look like this:

$$\boxed{115}$$

> *It's important to note:*
>
> While directions to the exercises are included in this workbook, the explanations and examples are not. To fully understand the activity, remember to read the text in *Career Choices* before you begin the exercise.
>
> In addition, when the workbook directions refer to a page number or resource, this citation corresponds to the page number in *Career Choices*. Be sure to look up these pages in *Career Choices*, not in the *Workbook and Portfolio*.

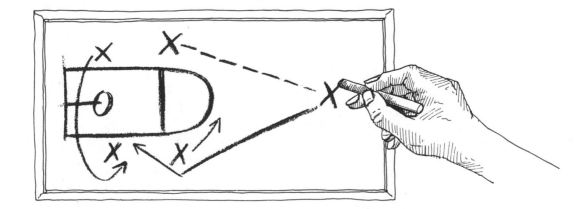

Getting the Most Out of This Experience

Your Career Portfolio Notebook

Your Career Portfolio Notebook is created *by you* using selected activities in this workbook, along with documents, photos, and projects you've completed. The specific activities are identified with this logo. For details, turn to page 126 of this workbook.

My10yearplan.com®

Your instructor may choose to use this optional online tool. My10yearPlan.com provides you with your own personal online planning area where you can enter the information from the activities with this logo, making it easy to store and update the data related to your 10-year plan. Depending on the version your instuctor selects and your access to computers, you may be entering your data daily, weekly, or even at the end of your course. See pages 128–131 of this workbook for more information.

Checkpoints

We all like to know how we are doing and what we get in return for the energy we put into a project. To help you answer these questions, we've provided Checkpoints for self-assessment. Beginning on page 132 of this workbook, the checkpoints are simple statements that describe the benefits of your efforts. Some people will first read through the statements before they begin each chapter and others will wait until after they've experienced the material to evaluate their comprehension. Choose the strategy that works best for you. You don't want to miss out on any of the important concepts covered, and this easy self-assessment process will help you stay on track. After all, your future happiness and life satisfaction are at stake.

Vocabulary of Success

The words you use to communicate your thoughts, ideas, knowledge, and feelings, both on the job and in your relationships, say a lot about who you are. At the beginning of each chapter of this workbook is a list of some important words from the corresponding chapter of *Career Choices*. Review them and write their definitions before reading the chapter. Then, when you come across these words as you read the main textbook, they will be more meaningful. You will also start building a vocabulary that will impress not only your friends and family but also potential employers, college recruiters, and future co-workers.

Chapter 1

Vocabulary of Success

elaborate _____

gamut _____

vision _____

realization _____

frustration _____

security _____

discrimination _____

achievement _____

fanatic _____

excess _____

flaunt _____

prima donna _____

integrity _____

humility _____

intuition _____

impulsive _____

procrastination _____

compliant _____

rational _____

interchangeable _____

VISION + ENERGY = SUCCESS

What do you think are the real stories behind the successful people we talked about on the pages 10–11? For the following exercises, write a statement that you feel might reflect his or her vision. Then list some actions they may have taken to realize their goal.

Complete charts for the following individuals.

Sally Ride

Vision: _____

Actions in school: _____

Actions at work: _____

Oprah Winfrey

Vision: _____

Actions in school: _____

Actions at work: _____

Barack Obama

Vision: _____

Actions in school: _____

Actions at work: _____

Your Portfolio and 10-Year Plan

There are a number of activities in this book that, once you complete them, you will want to include in your portfolio or your online 10-year plan. This individual data, along with your personal reflections, will be vital to the success of your career and life planning process over the next few years. You'll want this information readily available when meeting with school counselors, career advisors, and mentors, as well as when preparing for job or college interviews. See pages 126–131 for details.

Envisioning *Your* Future

14

What about you? Do you have a vision for your own future? You need to begin imagining one, if you don't. It's an important first step. Once you have a vision, you start expecting to realize it. What you expect for yourself tends to become what you get. So imagine a *positive* future for yourself.

Sit quietly, close your eyes, and imagine your ideal career. What kind of setting are you in? What tasks are you performing? Are you working alone or with others? How do you feel about yourself? Describe your vision in as much detail as possible.

_____

_____

_____

_____

_____

_____

_____

_____

_____

_____

Everybody Works

Whether you currently earn money from a job or not, you are a worker. You are probably a student. Chances are you do chores at home. Perhaps you are an athlete or a musician, a computer whiz or a video fanatic, a cook or a gardener. For the purpose of this exercise, consider all your studies, tasks, and hobbies as work.

Think about a typical "working day," one in which you spent time on most of your "jobs." List the tasks and activities you performed below. Make your list as complete as you can.

_____

_____

_____

Based on that list, how would you define your jobs? Write your titles on the following lines.

I am a _____

_____

_____

What would be your accomplishments at the end of the day (an English paper, a clean room, a solved problem, and so on)? List them below.

_____

_____

_____

Which accomplishments are most satisfying? _____

_____

How do they make you feel about yourself? _____

_____

Do your feelings relate to any of the reasons people work listed on the previous page? Which ones?

_____

_____

Defining Success

What does success mean to you? What would make you feel that you are a successful human being? In addition to thinking about what you do, contemplate the type of person you want to be.

Other people have made their opinions known as well. We've listed some of them below. Do any of them match your definition? Indicate whether you strongly agree, agree, are not sure, disagree, or strongly disagree with each statement.

	Strongly Agree	Agree	Not Sure	Disagree	Strongly Disagree
Money, achievement, fame, and success are important, but they are bought too dearly when acquired at the cost of health. — Anonymous					
It's great to be great, but it's better to be human. — Will Rogers					
Nothing succeeds like excess. — Oscar Wilde					
Success is a journey, not a destination. — Ben Sweetland					
The fastest way to succeed is to look as if you're playing by other people's rules, while quietly playing by your own. — Michael Korda					
She could not separate success from peace of mind. The two must go together... — Daphne Du Maurier, *Mary Anne*					
All of us are born for a reason, but all of us don't discover why. Success in life has nothing to do with what you gain in life or accomplish for yourself. It's what you do for others. — Danny Thomas					
I've never sought success in order to get fame and money; it's the talent and the passion that count in success. — Ingrid Bergman					
The two leading recipes for success are building a better mousetrap and finding a bigger loophole. — Edgar A. Shoaff					
Success is something to enjoy—to flaunt! Otherwise, why work so hard to get it? — Isobel Lennart, *Funny Girl*					
Success is knowing what your values are and living in a way consistent with your values. — Danny Cox					
Success can only be measured in terms of distance traveled... — Mavis Gallant					
If at first you don't succeed, you are running about average. — M.H. Anderson					
I think success has no rules, but you can learn a great deal from failure. — Jean Kerr, *Mary, Mary*					

	Strongly Agree	Agree	Not Sure	Disagree	Strongly Disagree
Success can make you go one of two ways. It can make you a *prima donna,* or it can smooth the edges, take away the insecurities, let the nice things come out. — Barbara Walters					
Six essential qualities that are the key to success: Sincerity, personal integrity, humility, courtesy, wisdom, charity. — Dr. William Menninger					
The people who try to do something and fail are infinitely better than those who try to do nothing and succeed. — Lloyd Jones					
The wealthy man is the man who is much, not the one who has much. — Karl Marx					
Winning isn't everything—it's the only thing. — Vince Lombardi					
Only those who dare to fail greatly can ever achieve greatly. — Robert F. Kennedy					
If at first you don't succeed, try, try again. Then give up. There's no use being a fool about it. — W. C. Fields					
I'm opposed to millionaires, but it would be dangerous to offer me the position. — Mark Twain					

19

Making Career Choices

20

Which of these patterns do you use most often? Explain.

_____

_____

Your Definition of Sucess

21

Write your own definition of success here:

_____

_____

_____

My
10yearPlan
.com

_____
your name

9

Chapter 2

Vocabulary of Success

aesthetic _____

forthright _____

forceful _____

authoritative _____

influencing _____

spontaneous _____

amiable _____

methodical _____

analytical _____

meticulous _____

diplomatic _____

systematic _____

submissive _____

charismatic _____

empathy _____

innovative _____

perseverance _____

versatile _____

synthesize _____

negotiate _____

Your Personal Profile

Write your name in the center of the chart, then add as many words as you can that describe your own passions, values, strengths, and so forth. As you fill out your chart, keep in mind that everyone has many different sides. Don't worry if some of your answers seem incompatible with others.

Your name

Passions

Values

Personality and
Strengths

Skills and
Aptitudes

Roles, Occupations,
and Vocations

Identifying Your Passions

These are some of the items on Letitia's list:

Winning a debate	Chocolate	Red shoes
Dancing	The Lakers	Long walks
Texting	Social justice	*The Star-Spangled Banner*
Politics	Movies that make me cry	Writing

Complete the following statements. Don't be frustrated if you can't do it immediately. But start being aware of these feelings. As more ideas occur to you in the next weeks, turn back to this page and add them to your lists. You will continue to discover new passions throughout your life.

My heart pounds with excitement when . . .

_____

_____

I feel especially good about myself when . . .

_____

_____

I get a lump in my throat when . . .

_____

_____

I lose track of time whenever I am . . .

_____

_____

If I could be any person in history, I would be . . .

_____

_____

When I dream about my future, I see myself . . .

_____

_____

If I could change one thing about the world, it would be . . .

_____

_____

WORK VALUES SURVEY

What are *your* values? Is having plenty of time to spend with friends and family important to you? Or would you rather be off on some kind of adventure? Do you want to help other people? Do you want to exercise power? The following exercise should give some indication of what you value most. For each statement below, check the column that comes closest to matching your feelings.

	Very True	Some-Times True	Not Sure	Not True
1. I'd rather donate to a good cause than join a prestigious club.				
2. I'd rather have good friends than a lot of money.				
3. I'd rather have my savings in a bank account than in the stock market.				
4. I'm too adventurous to be tied down by a family.				
5. I'd like a job where I set my own hours.				
6. I enjoy books and movies where the moral to the story is not obvious.				
7. I'd rather be a scholar than a politician.				
8. I would not want to work while my children are young.				
9. I would rather write a fictional story than a research paper.				
10. When I lend money to a friend, I don't worry about being paid back.				
11. I'd rather be famous than wealthy.				
12. I would rather associate with influential people than intellectual people.				
13. Teachers should be paid as much as business executives.				
14. I'd rather go to an art museum than a sporting event.				
15. I will contribute to my retirement account before I buy extras.				
16. I prefer jobs where the duties are varied and challenging.				
17. I prefer jobs where the duties are consistent and goals are clear.				
18. I feel a person's salary indicates how much he or she is valued on the job.				
19. I would not want a high-powered job because it could strain my marriage.				
20. It is important to me that my surroundings are attractive.				
21. My reputation is worth more to me than all the money in the world.				
22. I'd rather visit a place than read about it.				
23. I'd rather know something than be *known for* something.				
24. I'd rather have a secure job than a powerful one.				
25. I'd like to be my own boss.				
26. I believe a percentage of my income should be used to help others.				
27. I would turn down a promotion if it meant I had to travel away from my family too much.				

	Very True	Some-Times True	Not Sure	Not True
28. "Money talks."				
29. I would take a cut in salary if I were offered a position in the President's Cabinet.				
30. I'd rather own a special work of art than a fancy car.				
31. I'd rather have time than money.				
32. I will always stop to watch a beautiful sunset.				
33. If my brother committed a crime, I would turn him in.				
34. I don't like to do things the same way all the time.				
35. My friendships are more precious to me than possessions.				
36. The fact that most careers that "help others" make lower wages would not stop me from entering these lines of work.				
37. It is important that I get recognition for what I do.				
38. I'd rather *work* for an exciting company than *run* a dull one.				
39. I would like to run for office in my community.				
40. I'd rather work for someone else than have my own business.				
41. The first thing I would consider when deciding on a career is how much it pays.				
42. I always take time to be a good friend.				
43. The mundane work of feeding the hungry or caring for the sick would not bother me.				
44. I don't like my decisions questioned.				
45. I'd rather have a job with a high income than one with a lot of security.				
46. It is important for me to understand how things work.				
47. I like to organize the activities of my friends and family.				
48. If I were famous, I would enjoy signing autographs.				
49. I'd rather have a secure job than an exciting one.				
50. Owning nice things is important to me.				
51. I like to do things my own way.				
52. I feel good when I volunteer my time to make my community a better place.				
53. I would never testify in court against someone in my family.				
54. It is important to me that my home is beautiful.				
55. I like to be in charge.				
56. I would rather work together with other people than alone.				
57. Books and reading are important to me.				
58. I would stand up for my beliefs even if I were punished for it.				
59. I like to solve problems.				
60. I expect to be consulted when a group I am in is making a decision.				
61. If I believed strongly in a "cause," I would make it my first priority.				
62. I have expensive tastes.				
63. If a member of my family committed a crime, I would turn him or her in to the appropriate authorities.				
64. I don't like my friends to be too dependent on me.				
65. I'd rather be married than single.				

32

	Very True	Some-Times True	Not Sure	Not True
66. I like to make things.				
67. My appearance is important to me.				
68. I'd love to travel around the world alone.				
69. I am sensitive to colors that clash.				
70. Someday I'd like to own my own business.				
71. I'd rather be a leader than a follower.				
72. I'd rather follow someone else.				
73. I like to learn something new everyday.				
74. I would never marry someone who had less money than I do.				
75. It is important that my mate is good looking.				
76. I would borrow money to go on a vacation.				
77. Charity begins at home.				
78. With enough money, I could be happy.				
79. I think it would be exciting to be famous.				
80. I value my privacy...I wouldn't want to be famous.				
81. I believe I should be home every night with my family and not out with friends.				
82. "Don't rock the boat."				
83. I would not take a job that I felt was unethical, no matter how much money it paid.				
84. I enjoy people who do things differently.				
85. I will go out of my way to help a stranger.				
86. I would like to have a building or street named after me.				
87. I would not lie even if telling the truth might hurt a friend's reputation.				
88. I'd rather live in a cabin in the wilderness than a beautiful home.				
89. I like to look at problems from many different angles.				
90. It is important to me to be an influential person.				
91. I'd like to be known as being one of the best in my field.				
92. I like to try new things.				
93. I will not change my views just because they're unpopular.				
94. I think you should question "rules" if they don't make sense to you.				
95. I wouldn't want to travel alone.				
96. If asked, I would serve Thanksgiving dinner to the homeless and miss my family's celebration.				
97. I always stand up for what I believe in.				
98. I wouldn't like doing the same task all day long.				
99. I like to be called in an emergency.				
100. My family will be more important to me than my career.				
101. Trophies and awards are important to me.				
102. I like to help friends with their problems.				
103. My title at work is very important to me.				
104. It is important to share my life with someone.				

33

Now, assign a numerical value to each of your answers. Statements in the "very true" column are worth 9 points. Those you marked "sometimes true" get 6 points. Allow 3 points for each "not sure," and zero points for every "not true" answer.

In the columns on this page, write the numerical value of your response next to the statement number. For example, if you answered "very true" to the first statement, you would write a 9 on the line next to the number 1. When you have entered a number on each line, go back and total the columns under each heading.

ANSWERS

ADVENTURE	FAMILY	POWER	RECOGNITION	HELPING OTHERS
4. _____	8. _____	12. _____	11. _____	1. _____
16. _____	19. _____	29. _____	37. _____	26. _____
22. _____	27. _____	39. _____	48. _____	36. _____
38. _____	53. _____	47. _____	79. _____	43. _____
68. _____	65. _____	55. _____	86. _____	52. _____
76. _____	77. _____	60. _____	91. _____	85. _____
88. _____	81. _____	71. _____	101. _____	96. _____
92. _____	100. _____	90. _____	103. _____	99. _____
Total _____	Total _____	Total _____	Total _____	Total _____

PERSONAL INTEGRITY & MORAL COURAGE	FRIENDSHIP & COMPANIONSHIP	KNOWLEDGE & TRUTH	BEAUTY & AESTHETICS	INDEPENDENCE & FREEDOM
21. _____	2. _____	7. _____	14. _____	5. _____
33. _____	10. _____	13. _____	20. _____	25. _____
44. _____	35. _____	23. _____	30. _____	31. _____
58. _____	42. _____	46. _____	32. _____	51. _____
63. _____	56. _____	57. _____	54. _____	64. _____
83. _____	95. _____	61. _____	67. _____	70. _____
93. _____	102. _____	73. _____	69. _____	80. _____
97. _____	104. _____	87. _____	75. _____	94. _____
Total _____	Total _____	Total _____	Total _____	Total _____

CREATIVITY	MONEY	SECURITY
6. _____	18. _____	3. _____
9. _____	28. _____	15. _____
34. _____	41. _____	17. _____
59. _____	45. _____	24. _____
66. _____	50. _____	40. _____
84. _____	62. _____	49. _____
89. _____	74. _____	72. _____
98. _____	78. _____	82. _____
Total _____	Total _____	Total _____

In which category did you have the highest total? Right now, that value is most important to you. Remember, though, that values often change over time. You might want to come back to this survey every year or so when you are considering a change in your plans.

Did you have high scores in more than one category? If so, you might want to try to find a career that satisfies both or all your top values. If you value both beauty and adventure, for example, you might be happier tracking down international jewel thieves than you would be working in an art gallery or museum.

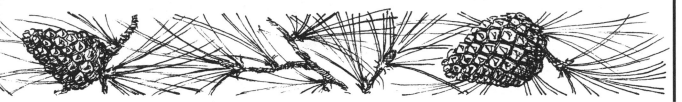

Strengths and Personality

In the four columns below, you will find a list of personality traits. Circle the 10 traits you feel best describe you.

a.	b.	c.	d.
forthright	enthusiastic	steady	analytical
adventurous	expressive	amiable	controlling
forceful	influencing	predictable	perfectionist
sharp	emotional	supportive	systematic
decisive	inventive	loyal	conventional
risk taker	spontaneous	methodical	respectful
demanding	trusting	team player	meticulous
authoritative	outgoing	calm	well-disciplined
direct	unselfish	thorough	diplomatic
curious	self-assured	dependable	precise
competitive	charming	self-composed	sensitive
self-sufficient	inspiring	possessive	accurate

Now total the number circled in each column.

_____   _____   _____   _____

Total from column a   Total from column b   Total from column c   Total from column d

41

Complete the following self-evaluation quiz. Circle the letter under each situation that best reflects how you would be likely to act, feel, or think.

1. Your favorite projects are ones that are
   a. likely to have favorable results.
   b. enjoyable to take part in.
   c. clearly explained.
   d. detail oriented.

2. You are on the community hospital's fund-raising committee. You would be happiest
   a. chairing the committee.
   b. publicizing the event and selling tickets.
   c. decorating the hall.
   d. keeping track of the monies collected.

3. When doing a task, you
   a. complete it in the shortest time possible.
   b. allow interruptions to take phone calls from friends.
   c. are willing to take time to help another student with their assignment.
   d. take time to check all your work for accuracy and thoroughness.

4. When faced with a stressful situation, you
   a. take charge and sometimes override the decisions of others.
   b. confront and may act in an impulsive fashion.
   c. become submissive and allow others to make your decisions.
   d. resist change and withdraw from the situation.

5. When getting dressed in the morning, you
   a. know exactly what you want to wear without giving it much thought.
   b. try on three things before deciding which is best.
   c. put on the clothes you laid out the night before.
   d. have no problem coordinating outfits because everything in your closet is in color sequence.

6. Your family is moving across the country to a lovely new home. You feel
   a. excited.
   b. curious.
   c. cautious.
   d. worried.

7. When you ask someone a question about a problem, you like an answer that
   a. is direct and to the point.
   b. includes stimulating ideas on various ways the problem could be solved.
   c. outlines the process for solving the problem.
   d. includes data and background on how the solution was reached.

8. When solving a problem, you are
   a. decisive.
   b. spontaneous.
   c. considered.
   d. deliberate.

9. When going shopping for clothes, you
   a. will not need a list. If you forget something, you'll just get it later.
   b. buy whatever catches your eye. You don't worry how different outfits go together.
   c. have a list and visit every store in town before finalizing your purchases.
   d. know exactly what you want and have searched the mall web site for sales.

Information on personality styles is adapted from the widely-used DiSC™ Dimensions of Behavior model and the *Personal Profile System*® assessment instrument, ™ copyright 1972, Carlson Learning Company. Used with permission of Carlson Learning Company, Minneapolis, Minnesota.

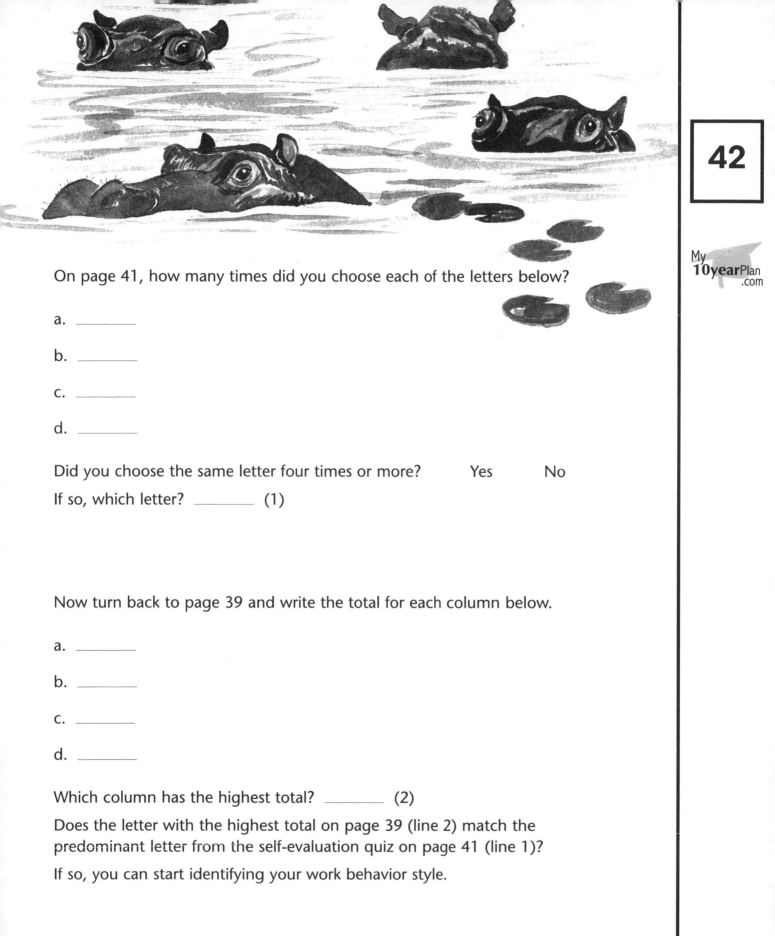

On page 41, how many times did you choose each of the letters below?

a. _____

b. _____

c. _____

d. _____

Did you choose the same letter four times or more?　　Yes　　No

If so, which letter? _____ (1)

Now turn back to page 39 and write the total for each column below.

a. _____

b. _____

c. _____

d. _____

Which column has the highest total? _____ (2)

Does the letter with the highest total on page 39 (line 2) match the predominant letter from the self-evaluation quiz on page 41 (line 1)?

If so, you can start identifying your work behavior style.

Your Strengths

44

What are your strengths?

_____

_____

_____

_____

_____

45

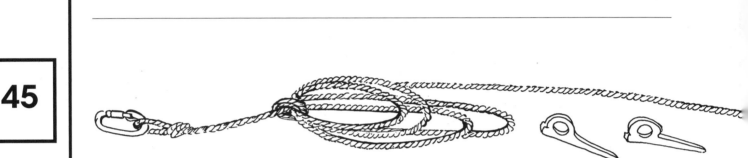

Now complete the chart below. Choose ten of the personal strengths you have identified and list them in the first column. Then, in the second column, describe a situation or personal experience where you used these strengths or where they might be helpful.

I AM:	I HAVE USED THIS STRENGTH TO:
1.	
2.	
3.	
4.	
5.	
6.	
7.	
8.	
9.	
10.	

Name That Skill

Use the following exercise to begin a list of specific skills you've mastered. Write three accomplishments that gave you the most satisfaction, or that you're most proud of, on the lines below. Then, in the middle column, list the skills you used in that enterprise. If you have a hard time identifying these skills, describe the experience to friends or family members and ask them to help you. (You'll complete the last column next.)

Accomplishment	Skills Required	Skills Category*
1.		
2.		
3.		

Do you see any pattern in the kinds of skills you used?

* Basic Skills – Social Skills – Complex Problem Solving Skills – Technical Skills – Systems Skills – Resource Management Skills

Skills Identification

Each occupation requires a unique set of skills. Looking for common skill sets is one way of classifying jobs. Below are six broad **skill categories** used to group occupations on O*NET Online. Designed to group occupations that use the 35 general skills listed within these skill categories, you'll want to visit O*NET Online when you begin your research process in chapter six.

For now, review the list below and place a check mark next to each general skill that you feel competent in and an "X" next to those you want acquire in the future. Note: You're not required to select from more than one category of skills.

Basic Skills
- [ ] Reading Comprehension
- [ ] Active Listening
- [ ] Writing
- [ ] Speaking
- [ ] Mathematics
- [ ] Science
- [ ] Critical Thinking
- [ ] Active Learning
- [ ] Learning Strategies
- [ ] Monitoring

Social Skills
- [ ] Social Perceptiveness
- [ ] Coordination
- [ ] Persuasion
- [ ] Negotiation
- [ ] Instructing
- [ ] Service Orientation

Complex Problem Solving Skills
- [ ] Complex Problem Solving

Technical Skills
- [ ] Operations Analysis
- [ ] Technology Design
- [ ] Equipment Selection
- [ ] Installation
- [ ] Programming
- [ ] Operation Monitoring
- [ ] Operation and Control
- [ ] Equipment Maintenance
- [ ] Troubleshooting
- [ ] Repairing
- [ ] Quality Control Analysis

Systems Skills
- [ ] Judgment and Decision Making
- [ ] Systems Analysis
- [ ] Systems Evaluation

Resource Management Skills
- [ ] Time Management
- [ ] Management of Financial Resources
- [ ] Management of Material Resources
- [ ] Management of Personnel Resources

Within each of the skills listed above are more specific skills. For instance, your "repairing" skills may relate to computers or lawn movers or jet engines. Review your skills on page 47 and, in the far right column on that page, indicate which of the six skills categories relates to each one. Do you have a preference for any one skills category? If so, which one?

_____

Below list specific skills, expertise, or talents you currently have that are not listed on page 47.

_____	_____	_____
_____	_____	_____
_____	_____	_____

Can you think of skills you would like to learn but have not yet mastered? Expand the list above and be more specific. For instance, would you like to learn web design or contract negotiation, dog grooming or sales techniques?

_____	_____	_____
_____	_____	_____
_____	_____	_____

What messages have you received? For the following exercise, write what you think the significant people in your life would tell you about your future. Imagine them leaving their messages on your voicemail.

The Message Center

Hello, you have reached _____'s message center. What would you like to tell me about my future? BEEP!

Mother's message: _____

_____

Father's message: _____

_____

Teacher's message: _____

_____

Other significant adult's message (coach, mentor, boss, relative): _____

_____

_____

Best friend's message: _____

_____

Girlfriend or boyfriend's message: _____

_____

Society's message:

_____

_____

_____

Positive Messages to Yourself

What positive messages can you give yourself about your future? Write them below. Recite them to yourself often, or read them into a digital voice recorder and play them again and again while you're relaxing.

1. _____

_____

2. _____

_____

3. _____

_____

4. _____

_____

5. _____

_____

Chapter 3

Vocabulary of Success

self-actualization _____

esteem _____

survival _____

capable _____

necessity _____

satisfaction _____

hierarchy _____

legacy _____

acknowledgement _____

epitaph _____

lifestyle _____

sociology _____

psychology _____

component _____

contemplation _____

spiritual _____

recuperate _____

external _____

internal _____

priority _____

Where Are You Now?

Answer the following questions to determine your present location on the Maslow Triangle. If you answer yes to the questions in each section, color in the corresponding section on the triangle below.

SURVIVAL

Do you have enough food and water to survive?	Yes	No
Do you have a place to live?	Yes	No
Do you have enough clothes to keep you warm?	Yes	No

SECURITY AND SAFETY

Do you feel safe?	Yes	No
Do you feel secure?	Yes	No

SENSE OF BELONGING

Do you feel you belong somewhere?	Yes	No
Do you feel loved?	Yes	No

SELF-ESTEEM

Do you feel good about yourself?	Yes	No
Do you feel worthwhile or valuable as a human being?	Yes	No

SELF-ACTUALIZATION

Do you feel accomplished?	Yes	No
Do you feel mature?	Yes	No
Do you trust your judgment?	Yes	No
Do you feel in control of your life?	Yes	No

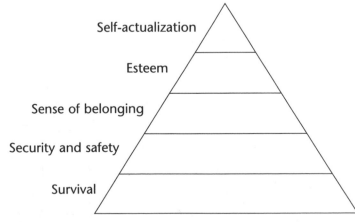

How Do You Want to be Remembered?

In the space below, write your own epitaph. How do you want to be remembered? At the end of your life, what would you have to have done in order to be thought of that way? You don't have to limit your answer to a single line, but keep it brief.

_____ : _____

Your Name

_____

_____

COMPONENTS OF LIFESTYLE

63

Lifestyle has many components. We've listed some below. Think about your ideal future life and complete this questionnaire as best you can.

RELATIONSHIPS

Do you want to be married? _____ Have children? _____ If so, how many? _____

What kinds of people would you like to be your friends? _____

_____

How much time (hours per week) will you want to spend with your family? Your friends?

_____

WORK

How much time do you want to spend at your chosen profession? Less than 20 hours per week? 20–40 hours per week? 40–50 hours? As long as it takes?

_____

What is your mission in life? What sort of commitment do you want or need to make to some larger goal?

_____

PERSONAL

How much time each week would you like to spend on:

Recreation _____ Individual pursuits _____ Contemplation and relaxation _____

How much flexibility do you want in your life? _____

What will be the "pace" of your life? Are you a high-energy person who always needs to have many projects at once, or are you a person who likes to tackle one thing at a time?

_____

How will you meet your spiritual needs? _____

MATERIAL ITEMS

Where do you want to live? Describe the location and housing. _____

_____

What income level would you like to reach? _____

Describe the possessions you want most. _____

_____

My
10yearPlan
.com

The Modified Maslow Triangle

When Joanie was 25, she had a financially secure job that she loved, the respect of her fellow workers, and a circle of devoted and loving friends. Shade the triangle below to represent the levels Joanie had attained in both her professional and personal life.

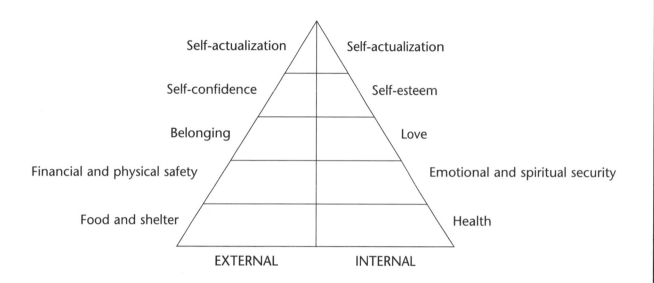

By the time she was 30, things had changed. Her job seemed less satisfying, though she put in many hours. The resulting stress caused health problems. Many of her friends had married and started families or moved away to take new jobs, and Joanie's social life dramatically changed. She thought she might like to have a family of her own, but she wasn't dating anyone at the moment. Shade this triangle to show how Joanie's life had changed.

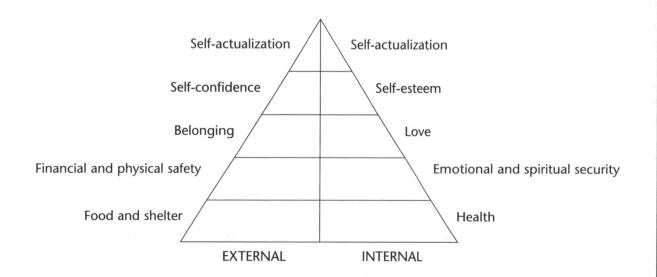

What About Your Life?

Shade the triangle below to show the balance in your life right now. Do you need to make any adjustments? What could you do to make your life more satisfying?

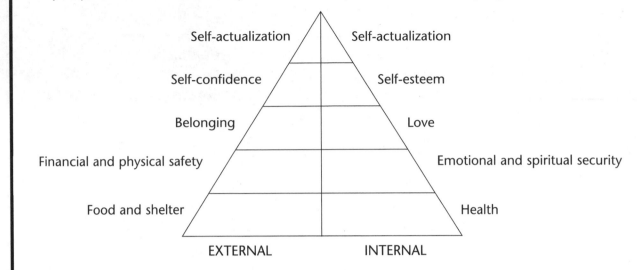

Now interview one of your parents or another adult you know and interpret his or her responses to the above questions. Shade the triangle below to show his or her balance.

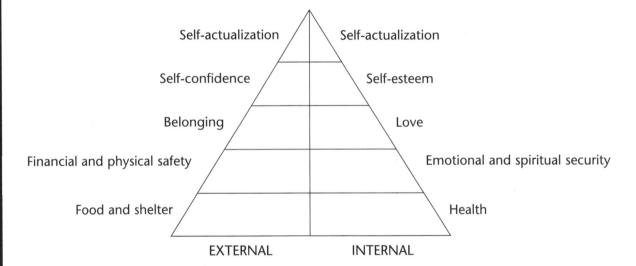

What do you think the triangle of a homeless person living alone would look like?

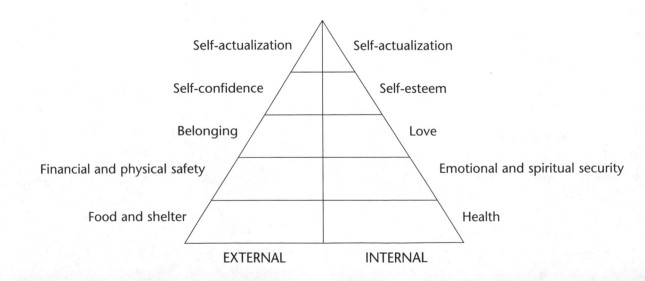

Chapter 4

Vocabulary of Success

privacy _____

commitment _____

profile _____

widow _____

aristocrat _____

affordability _____

variable _____

extensive _____

liberal _____

reallocate _____

poverty _____

conscious _____

traits _____

minimum _____

windfall _____

arrogant _____

persistence _____

dividends _____

inducement _____

interpretation _____

Your Budget

My
10yearPlan
.com

Let's talk about the kind of lifestyle you want to have—and how much money it is likely to cost. The following exercise asks you to make choices about everything from where you'd like to live to the vacations you'd like to take. Charts are provided to show approximate costs for many choices. Better yet, the Internet is a wonderful financial resource tool. The calculators and information available online will help you customize your budget to the penny. Once you make your choices in each category, enter your monthly expense in the space provided.

Since the point of the exercise is to help you make career decisions for your future, don't base your choices on what you think is realistic for you right now. Instead, think of the way you would like to be living at some specific age. (Make it at least 29 years old.)

Choose an age and then complete this statement: Today, I am _____ years old.
In _____ years, when I am _____ years old, this is how I would like my life to look.

FAMILY PROFILE

The first choice you need to make concerns your future family. In the real world, this choice is not totally under your control; for now, dream away. Check the marital status you see for yourself at the age you've chosen, and indicate the number of children you'll have, if any. Fill in the ages of your children.

MARITAL STATUS	CHILDREN	AGES OF CHILDREN
☐ Single	0 _____	_____
☐ Married	1 _____	_____
☐ Divorced	2 _____	_____
☐ Separated	3 _____	_____
☐ Widowed	4 _____	_____
☐ Other	5 _____	_____
	6 _____	_____

OTHER DEPENDANTS

_____

_____

_____

_____

WHERE I WOULD LIKE TO LIVE

_____

_____

WHY?

_____

_____

Housing

My
10yearPlan
.com

Housing is the most expensive item on most people's budget. It is possible that your future spouse, a titled aristocrat, will inherit the family estate (tax-free, of course). But don't count on it. For the purpose of this exercise, assume that you will have to allot a portion of your income for a place to live.

Keep your own values in mind as you complete this exercise. It's *your* dreams we're interested in, not your mom's or your best friend's.

Do you want to live in:

☐ Government housing   ☐ A farm or ranch

☐ A rental apartment   ☐ A cabin

☐ A cooperative apartment   ☐ A luxury home/estate

☐ A rental house   ☐ No permanent home

☐ Your own home   ☐ Other _____

☐ A condominium

How many bedrooms? _____ Bathrooms? _____

Other distinguishing features _____

_____

Check the classified advertisement section of a newspaper or a local realtor's web site to get an idea of the sales price of homes and rental rates. The charts on the next page may help you figure your monthly costs.

Monthly payment/rent	$ _____
Monthly property taxes	$ _____
Monthly insurance	$ _____
Total utilities/phone	$ _____
Housing	$ _____ [1]

Enter at [1] on page 42, Your Budget Profile,
of this workbook.

Transportation

Before you choose the kind of transportation you'll want or need, think about where you said you'd like to live. In some cities, it's quite easy to walk or use public transportation. In some places, a vehicle is almost a necessity. Consider, too, your physical condition and your mechanical ability.

Do you want to get around by:

☐ Walking

☐ Bicycle

☐ Motorcycle

☐ Public transportation

☐ Your own car, previously owned

☐ Your own car, bought new every 7–8 years

☐ Your own car, bought new every 3–4 years

☐ Your own car, bought new every year

☐ Limousine

☐ Other _____

If you want to own your own car:

What make? _____ Model? _____ Year? _____

How many miles per month do you plan to drive? _____

Monthly car payments	$ _____
Gasoline	$ _____
Maintenance and insurance	$ _____
Public transportation	$ _____
Transportation	$ _____ [2]

Enter at [2] on page 42,
Your Budget Profile,
of this workbook.

Clothing

Think about how much money you feel would be a reasonable amount to spend each year on clothing for yourself and each member of your family. How do you prefer to come by your clothes? Do you want or need an extensive wardrobe, or will just the basics do? Don't forget to make allotments for shoes, bathing suits, and other items that may not come immediately to mind. Then answer the questions below.

For clothing, I plan to:

☐ Sew for the family

☐ Purchase thrift store or "vintage" clothing

☐ Buy from discount or outlet stores

☐ Always buy on sale

☐ Buy from department stores and boutiques

☐ Buy designer fashions

☐ Other _____

I would like to have:

☐ A minimum wardrobe

☐ A moderate-size wardrobe

☐ An extensive wardrobe

☐ What I want, when I want it

List each member of your family and his or her projected clothing budget:

Family Member	Annual Budget
_____	$ _____
_____	$ _____
_____	$ _____
_____	$ _____
_____	$ _____
_____	$ _____
Annual Family Total	$ _____

Divide this figure by 12 to get your monthly clothing budget.

Clothing $ _____ [3]

Enter at [3] on page 42, Your Budget Profile, of this workbook.

Food

Some years back, a TV commercial featured a well-known naturalist who asked that memorable question, "Ever eat a pine tree?" He went on to inform viewers that "Some parts are edible." Perhaps. But most of us have come to expect more sophisticated fare. Still, there's plenty of room for negotiation between grazing in the forest and living solely on steak and caviar. The government has defined four kinds of food plans, each of which supplies the necessary nutrients. The Thrifty Plan is based on low-cost foods (beans, rice), but these may be unappealing to some people and may take more time for preparation. The Moderate Plan offers a greater variety of foods. The Liberal Plan lets you buy whatever you want, regardless of the cost.

Would you like your diet to be based on:

☐ The Thrifty Plan   ☐ The Moderate Plan

☐ The Low-Cost Plan   ☐ The Liberal Plan

Do you have any special dietary habits that might increase your food budget (i.e., gourmet cooking is your hobby, you have a restricted diet)? The chart on page 85 may help you come up with an amount.

Food $ _____ [4]

Enter at [4] on page 42, Your Budget Profile, of this workbook.

Sundries

Sundries are all those little things you pick up at the grocery or drug store: Shampoo, deodorant, toilet paper, cleaning supplies, and the like. How much would you plan to spend on these items each month?

Sundries $ _____ [5]

Enter at [5] on page 42, Your Budget Profile, of this workbook.

Entertainment and Recreation

Although the following budget items are not necessary to sustain life, they do have an impact on your self-esteem and life satisfaction. Answer the following questions, remembering to consider your spouse and your children's needs as well.

Monthly Total

How many times/month will you eat at a restaurant? _____

What will your average bill be? $ _____

How much per month will be spent on meals out? $ _____

Would you like to entertain friends?

What would you spend per month? $ _____

Would you like to attend concerts, movies, plays, sports events, and the like?

What would you spend per month? $ _____

Will you download music or mobile apps? Subscribe to newspapers and magazines on your e-book reader?

How much a month would you like to spend? $ _____

Will you have hobbies or take part in sports that cost money?

What? _____

How much will you need a month? $ _____

If you have children, what kinds of recreational/educational opportunities do you want for them? (Check their ages again.)

What? _____

How much will be spent per month? $ _____

One more consideration: Do you want to have special equipment related to entertainment or recreation? Would you like to have a laptop or tablet computer, MP3 player, gaming system, HDTV, musical instrument, boat, plane, country club or health club membership?

What do you want to spend on them per month? $ _____

Total entertainment $ _____ [6]

Enter at [6] on page 42, Your Budget Profile,
of this workbook.

No portion of this book may be photocopied or reproduced electronically without written permission from the publisher.

37

Vacations

This is not so much a "whether or not" budget item as it is a "where and how often" expenditure. It's been shown that taking time off is an important part of maintaining good physical and mental health. How do you want to do it?

Do you want to take a vacation:

☐ Monthly

☐ Every six months

☐ Yearly

☐ Every two years

☐ Every three to five years

☐ Other _____

What kind of vacation would you like to be able to afford:

☐ Car trip to relatives

☐ Camping/hiking

☐ Day trips to local amusements

☐ A week at the seashore or mountain cabin

☐ Car trips to places of interest

☐ Plane trips to places of interest

☐ Foreign travel

☐ Cruises, travel packages, or exotic clubs

☐ Other _____

☐ Other _____

☐ Other _____

What will you want to budget every year to meet your vacation objectives?

$ _____

Divide that figure by 12 to come up with your monthly figure.

Vacation $ _____ [7]

Enter at [7] on page 42, Your Budget Profile, of this workbook.

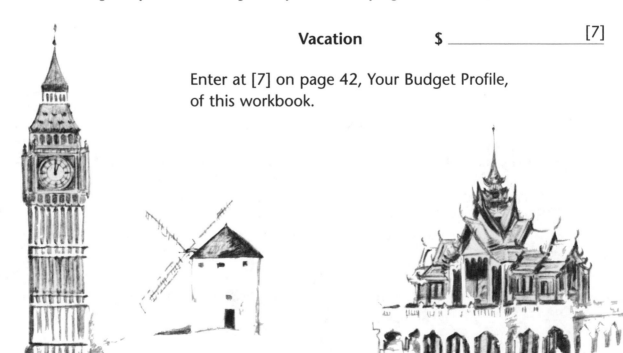

Child Care

If both parents are working while there are young children in the family (a reasonable assumption), you will need to consider your child care options. First, look back to see how many children you are planning to have, and their ages.

Would you have:

☐ No need for child care

☐ A relative to care for them

☐ A cooperative arrangement with a relative or friend

☐ Care in a community-based center

☐ A private nursery school or day care center

☐ A sitter coming into your home

☐ Live-in help

My
10yearPlan
.com

NATIONAL AVERAGE CHILD CARE COSTS	
Babysitter (in home, non-relative) Source: U.S. Census Bureau	$9.25/hour
Average Weekly Child Care Costs at Child Care Center	
Infant	$172.57
4-year-old child	$137.60
School-age child	$94.96

Source: Figures extrapolated from state averages, National Association of Child Care Resources & Referral Agencies, 2008 Price of Child Care, March 2009.

How much will this cost per child, per month?

child one $ _____

child two $ _____

child three $ _____

Total child care costs $ _____ [8]

Enter at [8] on page 42, Your Budget Profile, of this workbook.

DEPENDANT CARE

If you indicated at the beginning of this exercise that you plan to care for a dependant other than your children (a parent or grandparent, for example) remember to add that into your monthly budget. What do you plan to spend on dependant care? $ _____

What if there is a divorce of separation in your future? Will you need to pay alimony or child support? How much? $ _____ Keep these costs in mind as you plan for monthly reserves.

Health Care

Because an unforeseen accident or illness can play havoc with the most carefully planned budget, health insurance is a must. Many employers will subsidize your health insurance. But usually you will have to pay a portion of the cost. What kind of care do you want?

☐ Government-subsidized free clinics   ☐ Private physician and dentist

☐ Health Maintenance Organization care

See page 94 for some sample annual costs. Divide your projected annual costs by 12 months.

Health Care $ _____ [9]

Enter at [9] on page 42, Your Budget Profile, of this workbook.

Furnishings

You probably need to purchase replacement equipment and items for your home, such as linens, appliances, furniture, and decorative items. What about computer or home entertainment equipment? Assume you have most of these items by this time.

Annual budget $ _____ divided by 12.

Furnishings $ _____ [10]

Enter at [10] on page 42, Your Budget Profile, of this workbook.

Savings

This is an important part of any budget. There are predictable things to save for (a house, new furnishings, children's college, retirement) as well as things you'd rather not think about (losing your job, a major illness). It's not fun to spend money on a new roof or water heater, but sometimes it has to be done. And, it's a lot easier if you've planned for it. As a rule of thumb, every family should save at least six months' income in case of emergency.

What do you feel you should save each month for:

☐ Emergencies   ☐ Retirement

☐ Repairs, replacements, or major purchases   ☐ Income cushion

☐ Children's college

Savings $ _____ [11]

Enter at [11] on page 42, Your Budget Profile, of this workbook.

Miscellaneous

Are there things important to you that we haven't mentioned yet? Think about your values. Here are some possible additional expenses. Add your own if you need to.

What will be your monthly budget for holiday gifts and birthdays? $ _____

Will you have pets? If so, what kind? _____

How much per month will it cost to keep them? $ _____

Will you make contributions to social, political, or religious organizations?
If so, how much per month? $ _____

Do you want to send your children to private schools?   Yes   No   Undecided

How much will this cost per month? $ _____

Do you need an Internet connection, cable TV, cell phone, or other high tech services?

How much will this cost per month? $ _____

Other costs, list: _____ $ _____

_____ $ _____

_____ $ _____

Miscellaneous $ _____ [12]

Enter at [12] on page 42, Your Budget Profile,
of this workbook.

Your Budget Profile

Here's the moment of truth. Go through the exercise again and enter the monthly amounts you indicated in each category in the appropriate space below. Then add the column to come up with your total monthly budget.

[1] Housing $ _____

[2] Transportation $ _____

[3] Clothing $ _____

[4. Food $ _____

[5] Sundries $ _____

[6] Entertainment $ _____

[7] Vacations $ _____

[8] Child care $ _____

[9] Health care $ _____

[10] Furnishings $ _____

[11] Savings $ _____

[12] Miscellaneous $ _____

Total $ _____

What Salary Will Support this Lifestyle?

To find the monthly salary you will need to cover your expenses, divide your monthly expenses by 80 percent.

Expenses (or net pay) divided by 80% = Gross pay

_____ ÷ 80% = _____
Total from page 92   your required monthly salary

Multiply this figure by 12 (months) to get the annual salary figure required.

_____ x 12 = _____
your required monthly salary   your required annual salary

What Careers Support Your Lifestyle?

Make a list below of at least ten careers with average salaries that match your budget projections. For this activity, assume you are the sole "breadwinner" in your family.

CAREER TITLE AND AVERAGE SALARY   CAREER TITLE AND AVERAGE SALARY

_____   _____

_____   _____

_____   _____

_____   _____

_____   _____

HARD TIMES BUDGET

Did the figure for Your Budget Profile seem higher than the salary you're likely to earn on your own? What amount do you think you could reasonably expect to earn? Write that figure on line b below.

Next, determine your net income (line a), if you earn that salary (see formula on page 93), and reallocate your funds. Write the adjusted figures for your hard times budget below. The total should be a figure no larger than your *own* income. Don't count on your phantom spouse here.

1. Housing $ _____

2. Transportation $ _____

3. Clothing $ _____

4. Food $ _____

5. Sundries $ _____

6. Entertainment $ _____

7. Vacations $ _____

8. Child care $ _____

9. Health care $ _____

10. Furnishings $ _____

11. Savings $ _____

12. Miscellaneous $ _____

a) Net Income $ _____
(total amount you have to spend)

b) Gross monthly salary $ _____

43

WILL'S BUDGET

1. Housing	$ _____	8. Child care	$ _____
2. Transportation	$ _____	9. Health care	$ _____
3. Clothing	$ _____	10. Furnishings	$ _____
4. Food	$ _____	11. Savings	$ _____
5. Sundries	$ _____	12. Miscellaneous	$ _____
6. Entertainment	$ _____	**Net Income**	$ _____
7. Vacations	$ _____		

What is the gross monthly income required to come up with this net? $ _____

JEFF & FRANCIE'S BUDGET

1. Housing	$ _____	8. Child care	$ _____
2. Transportation	$ _____	9. Health care	$ _____
3. Clothing	$ _____	10. Furnishings	$ _____
4. Food	$ _____	11. Savings	$ _____
5. Sundries	$ _____	12. Miscellaneous	$ _____
6. Entertainment	$ _____	**Net Income**	$ __3,300__
7. Vacations	$ _____		

What is the gross monthly income required to come up with this net? $ _____

CARL & RUTH'S BUDGET

1. Housing $ _____	8. Child care $ _____	**100**
2. Transportation $ _____	9. Health care $ _____	
3. Clothing $ _____	10. Furnishings $ _____	
4. Food $ _____	11. Savings $ _____	
5. Sundries $ _____	12. Miscellaneous $ _____	
6. Entertainment $ _____	**Net Income** $ ___11,500___	
7. Vacations $ _____		

What is the gross monthly income required to come up with this net? $ _____

BEN & LYNN'S BUDGET

1. Housing $ _____	8. Child care $ _____
2. Transportation $ _____	9. Health care $ _____
3. Clothing $ _____	10. Furnishings $ _____
4. Food $ _____	11. Savings $ _____
5. Sundries $ _____	12. Miscellaneous $ _____
6. Entertainment $ _____	**Net Income** $ ___3,190___
7. Vacations $ _____	

What is the gross monthly income required to come up with this net? $ _____

Could You Become a Poverty Statistic?

103

What do you think contributes to poverty in this country?

_____

_____

_____

What might cause you to become one of these statistics?

_____

_____

How can you prevent that from happening?

_____

_____

_____

107

LEON'S STORY

What are the sacrifices Leon must make?

_____

Which values do these sacrifices reflect?

_____

What are Leon's rewards?

_____

Which values do they reflect?

_____

Do you share Leon's values?   Yes   No   Undecided

Are you willing to make the same sacrifices?   Yes   No   Undecided

VINCENT'S STORY

What are the sacrifices Vincent has made?

_____

Which values do they reflect?

_____

What are Vincent's rewards?

_____

Which values do they reflect?

_____

Do you share Vincent's values?   Yes   No   Undecided

Would you be ready to make similar sacrifices?

SARA'S STORY

Yes   No   Undecided

What sacrifices has Sara had to make? _____

_____

_____

What values categories would you put them under? _____

_____

_____

List Sara's rewards. _____

_____

_____

To which values categories do they belong? _____

_____

Do you and Sara have similar values?   Yes   No   Undecided

Would you be willing to make the same sacrifices? Yes   No   Undecided

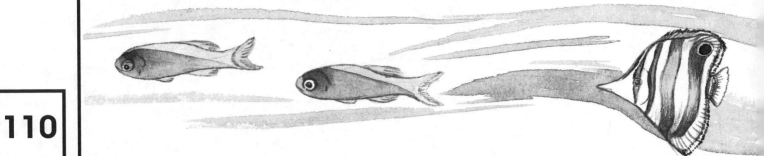

ROSE'S STORY

What sacrifices has Rose made for her career? _____

_____

What values categories would you place them in? _____

_____

What are her rewards? _____

_____

What values do you think they mirror? _____

_____

Are your values similar to Rose's?   Yes   No   Undecided

Would you make the same sacrifices?   Yes   No   Undecided

You Win Some, You Lose Some

Every job has its rewards and its sacrifices. How well a given career could work for you depends on your own values. It's important to recognize which values are compatible with a job and which are not. See how adept you are at recognizing which traits a job will call forth, and which it will deny. Review the values categories on pages 36 and 37. Then, for each of the following careers, list the values you think will be rewarded and those that will most likely be sacrificed.

Example: Career Military Officer

Rewards: Adventure

Sacrifices: Freedom, money or wealth

Computer programmer

Rewards: Security, creativity

Sacrifices: Beauty and aesthetics, adventure

Professional athlete

Rewards: Recognition, power, adventure

Sacrifices: Freedom, security

Fire fighter
Rewards: _____
Sacrifices: _____

Veterinarian
Rewards: _____
Sacrifices: _____

Fashion model
Rewards: _____
Sacrifices: _____

Radio announcer
Rewards: _____
Sacrifices: _____

Social worker
Rewards: _____
Sacrifices: _____

Mechanic
Rewards: _____
Sacrifices: _____

Farmer
Rewards: _____
Sacrifices: _____

Truck driver
Rewards: _____
Sacrifices: _____

Flight attendant
Rewards: _____
Sacrifices: _____

Homemaker
Rewards: _____
Sacrifices: _____

Garbage hauler
Rewards: _____
Sacrifices: _____

Accountant
Rewards: _____
Sacrifices: _____

Resort owner
Rewards: _____
Sacrifices: _____

After Hours Rewards

On each of the following lines, you'll find an occupation followed by a list of values. Circle those values you think would be met by the career. Then, on the line provided, state what this person might do to meet the other need.

Social worker: helping others creativity power _____

Assembly line worker: helping others security friendship _____

Carpenter: adventure beauty and aesthetics family _____

Sales representative: family money friendship _____

Homemaker: family helping others power _____

Museum guide: beauty and aesthetics adventure creativity _____

Professor: knowledge creativity recognition _____

Farmer: family helping others friendship _____

Psychologist: adventure helping others beauty and aesthetics _____

Accountant: power money creativity _____

Chemist: knowledge creativity recognition _____

Writer: creativity helping others friendship _____

Veterinarian: helping others knowledge power _____

An Investment in Education...
...Yields Dividends for a Lifetime

While it may not seem that $10,000 or $20,000 per year earning capacity is a big enough inducement to spend between three and 10 more years in school or in training, let's look at what that extra effort can mean over a lifetime.

The chart below shows more dramatically how each year of education affects future earnings.

How many years do you plan to work between the age of 18 and 65?

_____ years in workforce

Multiply the number of years you plan to be in the workforce with each of the annual salaries listed below to find out how much you would earn over the course of your working life.

$20,000 x _____ years in workforce = $ _____ lifetime earnings

$30,000 x _____ years in workforce = $ _____ lifetime earnings

$50,000 x _____ years in workforce = $ _____ lifetime earnings

$75,000 x _____ years in workforce = $ _____ lifetime earnings

$100,000 x _____ years in workforce = $ _____ lifetime earnings

What is the difference between a $20,000 and $30,000 annual salary over a lifetime? $ _____

What is the difference between a $20,000 and $50,000 annual salary over a lifetime? $ _____

What is the difference between a $20,000 and $75,000 annual salary over a lifetime? $ _____

What is the difference between a $20,000 and $100,000 annual salary over a lifetime? $ _____

What if you only earned minimum wage?

What is the current minimum wage rate per hour in your state or city? $ _____

How much can a person earn per year at that hourly rate? $ _____

What does that equal over your lifetime? $ _____

HOW DO YOU WANT TO SPEND YOUR TIME?

Maybe the time required to get the education and training for a job that interests you still seems too long, higher income or no. Let's look at it another way.

This bar graph represents an average lifespan—about 78 years. We've already filled it in for a high school graduate. That leaves you about 60 years to play around with. How will you spend that time?

Now envision your ideal future. How will you spend your time? Think about the kind of life you'd like to have, the job that appeals to you most, no matter how long the training required. Using the following directions as a guide, fill in the graph to age 78.

Using *polka dots,* fill in and label the block(s) of time for *post-high school training.*

Using *horizontal stripes,* fill in and label the block(s) of time for *working full-time* and diagonal lines for *working part-time.*

Using *stars,* fill in and label the block(s) of time *outside the workforce* for raising a family or retirement.

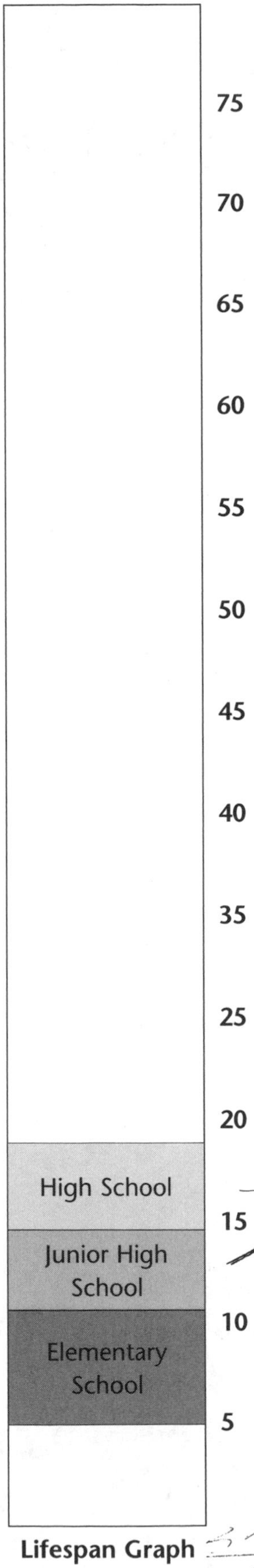

Lifespan Graph

75
70
65
60
55
50
45
40
35
25
20

High School

15

Junior High School

Elementary School

10

5

Use the information from your graph to answer the following questions.

How many years of post-high school training will you complete?

_____ years = a

How many years do you think you will work outside the home full-time?

_____ years = b

How many years do you think you will work outside the home part-time?

_____ years = c

Here are some interesting facts about your worklife.

How many hours might you work in your lifetime?

full-time   2,080 hours/year x _____ b = _____ f

part-time   1,000 hours/year x _____ c = _____ g

_____ f + _____ g = _____ hours you will work in your lifetime

That's a lot of time to be doing something that you do not find satisfying...that doesn't correspond to your values or passions...that doesn't meet your lifestyle desires.

Okay, let's look at it one more way.

For every year of post-high school education, you will work _____ years.

Hint: $\dfrac{b + c}{a} =$ _____ h

Next time you think, "I can't stay in school _____ more years! I didn't want to be a _____ anyway!" remember these figures. Education and training now are a small investment when you look at the long-range payoffs in life satisfaction. Hang in there...you'll be glad you did!

Ask Someone Who's Been There

The information in this book is necessarily more general than we'd like. You'll want to get specific answers to your questions. Interview three people (over age 29) in fields that interest you, adding their comments to your career resource files. The following questions will trigger a dialogue and lead to an in-depth understanding of each occupation.

NAME _____

OCCUPATION _____

HOW LONG IN THIS OCCUPATION? _____

How did you choose your occupation? _____

_____

Financially, does it let you live the way you prefer? _____

_____

If not, why not and what can you do about it? _____

_____

What rewards have you experienced? _____

> *(Listen carefully here. Keep the different values categories in mind.)*

    Values interpretation: _____

What sacrifices have you had to make for your career? _____

    Values interpretation: _____

What kind of commitment does this career take in terms of:

    Education _____

    Energy/endurance _____

    Stick-to-itiveness _____

If you had it to do over again, would you choose this career? _____

Why or why not? _____

Easier Said Than Done

Kay wants to save money for college. Her friend wants Kay to go with her on a ski vacation.

Jamal wants to do well at his weekend job. He feels like sleeping in on Saturday morning.

Lee wants to be in the school play. The thought of auditioning for a part makes him anxious.

Juanita wants to study art in France. Because of a scheduling problem, taking a French class would mean giving up her place in the school choir.

	It's easier to...	...than...	But what I want is...	...therefore, I will...
Kay Jamal Lee Juanita You				

Complete this chart for Kay, Jamal, Lee, and Juanita.

What do you want? Look back to the goals you set in chapter 3 and fill in the chart above. Use this model to help make day-to-day decisions about realizing your dreams.

Chapter 5

Vocabulary of Success

category _____
_____

characteristics _____
_____

environment _____
_____

frequent _____
_____

acquaintances _____
_____

isolation _____
_____

variety _____
_____

compatible _____
_____

flexible _____
_____

potential _____
_____

incentive _____
_____

option _____
_____

composite _____
_____

freelance _____
_____

sequential _____
_____

anxiety _____
_____

tolerance _____
_____

entrepreneur _____
_____

capital _____
_____

status _____
_____

On each of the next five pages, you will find a brief description of a particular category of career considerations. A list of options involving that category follows. Check the box in front of any statement that appeals to you. Choose as many options as you like, but make sure they don't contradict each other. Feel free to add to the lists if we've overlooked something that appeals to you..

Physical Settings

Check the statements that appeal to you below.

☐ I would like to work in a city.

☐ I would like to work in the country.

☐ I would like to work in a small to medium-sized town.

☐ I would like to work in _____ (list a specific city or part of the country).

☐ I would like to work in another country _____ .

☐ I would like a job that might offer frequent transfers.

☐ I would like a job that will let me stay in one place.

☐ I would like a job that keeps me "on the road," traveling from place to place.

☐ I would like to work outdoors (list specifics if you can, i.e., in the woods, on a farm, at sea) _____ .

☐ I would like to work out of a car or truck most of the time.

☐ I would like to work in an office.

☐ I would like to work in my home.

☐ It's important to me that my work setting be pleasing to the eye.

☐ I would like to work in a garage or warehouse.

☐ I would like to work in a factory.

☐ I would like a job that involves both indoor and outdoor work.

☐ I would like to work in a science lab or hospital.

☐ I would like to work in a retail store.

☐ I would like to work in a restaurant.

☐ I would like to work on a construction site.

☐ I would like to work on a ship, plane, train, or bus.

☐ I would like to work in a hotel or resort.

☐ I would like to work in a museum or art gallery.

☐ I would like to work in an art or photography studio.

☐ I would like to work in a concert hall or theater.

☐ I would like to work in a school or library.

☐ I would like to work in a church, synagogue, temple, or mosque.

☐ I would like to work on the set of a movie or TV show.

☐ I would like to work in a TV, radio, or recording studio.

☐ I would like to work in _____ .

Working Conditions

Check the statements below that appeal to you.

☐ I would like a job that requires me to "dress for success" (dress up for a professional office).

☐ I would like a job that requires me to wear a uniform or costume.

☐ I would like a job that lets me dress any way I want.

☐ I would like a job that lets me work alone most of the time.

☐ I would like a job that lets me work with the same group of people.

☐ I would like a job that lets me work with many different clients.

☐ I would like a job that lets me work with ideas.

☐ I would like a job that lets me work with information.

☐ I would like a job that lets me work with computers.

☐ I would like a job that lets me work with numbers.

☐ I would like a job that lets me work with machines.

☐ I would like a job that lets me work with tools.

☐ I would like a job that lets me be creative.

☐ I would like a job that involves physical labor or activity.

☐ I would like a job with prescribed duties and procedures.

☐ I would like a job with strict deadlines.

☐ I would like a job with structured working hours.

☐ I would like a job with somewhat flexible hours.

☐ I would like a job that lets me structure my time any way I want.

☐ I would like a job that often calls for putting in extra hours.

☐ I wouldn't mind working nights or weekends.

☐ I would like a job that involves risk or danger.

☐ I would like a job that might take away my privacy.

☐ I would like a job that is intellectually challenging.

☐ I would like a job I could forget about when I'm not there.

☐ I would like to be able to work part-time when my children are young.

☐ I would like a job that involves a variety of tasks and duties.

☐ Other _____

Relationships at Work

Check the statements below that appeal to you.

- ☐ I would like to work alone.
- ☐ I would like to work in a group or on a team.
- ☐ I would like to work with a variety of people.
- ☐ I would like to be the boss.
- ☐ I would like to be supervised by others.
- ☐ I would like to work for myself.
- ☐ I would like to work with adults.
- ☐ I would like to work with children.
- ☐ I would like to work with people fighting an illness.
- ☐ I would like to work with people with disabilities.
- ☐ I would like to work with older people.
- ☐ I would like to work with creative people.
- ☐ I would like to work with people like me.
- ☐ I would like to work with people different from me.
- ☐ I would like to work with people who speak a different language.
- ☐ I would like to work with people from underprivileged backgrounds.
- ☐ I would like to teach people.
- ☐ I would like to entertain people.
- ☐ I would like to make people feel better.
- ☐ I would like to make people look better.
- ☐ I would like to help people get out of trouble.
- ☐ I would like to sell things to people.
- ☐ I would like to work with people who are incarcerated.
- ☐ I would like to give people guidance.
- ☐ I would like to run for elected office.
- ☐ I would expect to socialize with my co-workers.
- ☐ I would like to meet celebrities on my job.
- ☐ I would like to work in a competitive environment.
- ☐ I would like a job where everyone works together for the common good.
- ☐ I would like to serve the public.
- ☐ I would like to serve private clients.
- ☐ Other _____

Psychological Rewards of Working

Check the statements below that appeal to you.

- ☐ I would like to be recognized in the community for the work I do.
- ☐ I would like a job where I am free to make my own decisions.
- ☐ I would like a job that furthers my mission in life.
- ☐ I would like a job that helps less fortunate members of the community.
- ☐ I would like a job that offers thrills and adventure.
- ☐ I would like a job that lets me put my family duties first.
- ☐ I would like a job in which I am continually learning something new.
- ☐ I would like a job that has high status in the community.
- ☐ I want to work with people I admire and respect.
- ☐ I would like a job that demands creativity and innovation.
- ☐ I would like to work for something I believe in, even if it is unpopular or puts me in danger.
- ☐ I would like a job that adds to the beauty in the world.
- ☐ I would like a job that adds to the safety of the world.
- ☐ I would like a position of power.
- ☐ I would like a job that gives me a lot of freedom.
- ☐ I want to feel secure that my job will be there as long as I want it.
- ☐ I would like to be applauded for my work.
- ☐ Other _____

Mixing Career and Family

Check the statements below that appeal to you.

- ☐ I want to be married.
- ☐ I want to have children.
- ☐ Family life is more important to me than my career.
- ☐ My career is more important to me than having a family.
- ☐ I would like both a rewarding career and a happy family life.
- ☐ I would like to stay home with my children when they are young.
- ☐ I would like my spouse to stay home with the children when they are young.
- ☐ I would like to work out of my house when my children are young.
- ☐ I would like a job with flexible hours so I can be available for my family.
- ☐ I would like to be able to afford to send my children to a daycare preschool.
- ☐ I would like to be able to afford to have a sitter come to the house.
- ☐ I would like to be able to afford to have live-in help with the children.
- ☐ I would like to be able to afford to have a housekeeper so I can spend more time with my family.
- ☐ I would expect my family to help out with household chores.
- ☐ Other _____

Financial Rewards

Check the statements below that appeal to you.

- ☐ I would like a job that pays at least $_____ per month. See page 93.
- ☐ I would like to be paid by the hour, with time and a half for overtime.
- ☐ I would like a monthly salary that doesn't vary with the number of hours I work.
- ☐ I would like to work on a commission basis.
- ☐ I would like a job that would be secure even in times of recession.
- ☐ I'm willing to accept a lower salary if the potential for either financial or psychological rewards is good.
- ☐ Money isn't important to me—I just need enough to get by.
- ☐ I want a job with good benefits (e.g., health insurance, pension plan, paid vacations, etc.).
- ☐ I'd like my salary to be based on my job performance.
- ☐ I'd like a job with scheduled pay increases.
- ☐ I'd like to be paid for the things I create or produce (e.g., paintings, articles, cookies, etc.).
- ☐ I'd like a job that offers bonuses or other incentives.
- ☐ I'm willing to start with a very low salary as long as there is an opportunity to work towards a very high salary.
- ☐ Other _____

Job Skills

This final category should help you fill out your general career outline. What are the skills you would most like to use on your job? Check back to chapter two and record your findings below.

My physical skills include: _____ _____

_____ _____ _____

My intellectual and creative skills include: _____

_____ _____ _____

My social skills include: _____ _____

_____ _____ _____

The skills I would like to acquire are:

_____ _____ _____

_____ _____ _____

_____ _____ _____

You will need to expand this list when you come up with a specific career goal.

Portfolio

134

My 10yearPlan.com

You probably checked a number of statements in each category. Read them all again to get a *very* broad picture of your career desires. Since it's unlikely that any job could meet all these requirements, go back and choose the one or two statements from each category that mean the most to you. Circle the boxes in front of those statements. Then enter them on the following chart. Keep these in mind as you begin shortening your list of possible careers.

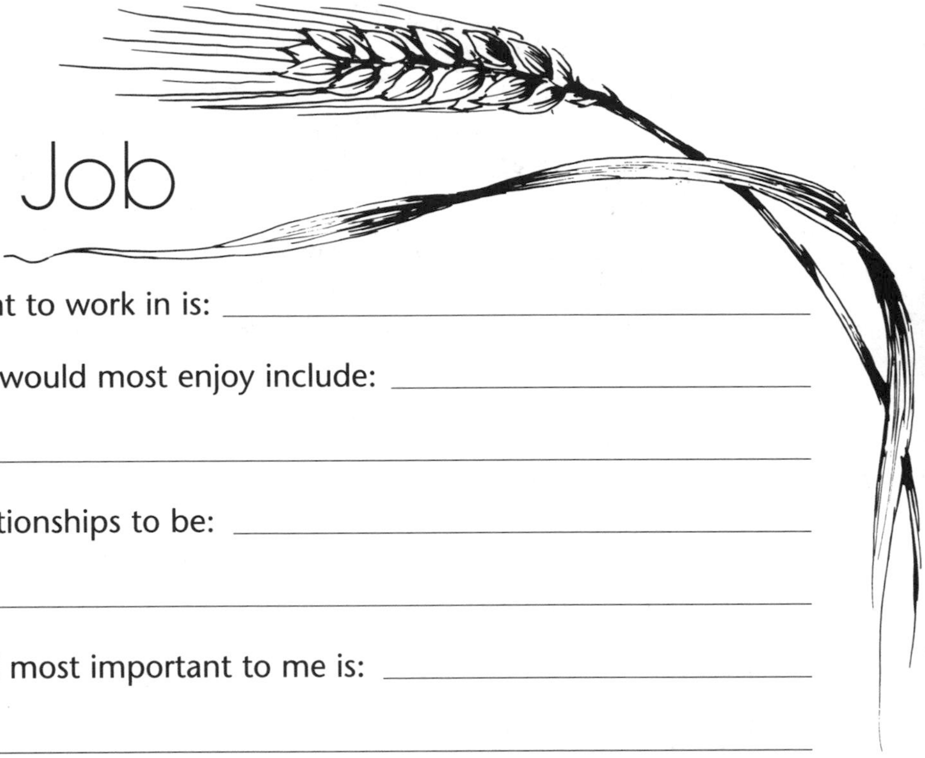

My Ideal Job

The physical setting I want to work in is: ______________________________

The working conditions I would most enjoy include: ______________________

____

I would like my work relationships to be: ______________________________

____

The psychological reward most important to me is: ______________________

____

My goals for mixing career and family include: __________________________

____

Financially, I would like: ____

____

The skills I have or would most like to acquire include: ___________________

____

Do your answers support any of the career choices you had in mind? Do they rule out any of them? Do they suggest new possibilities?

Job Characteristics

On the chart below, circle one job characteristic on each line that appeals most to you.

Column 1	Column 2
Full-time	Part-time
Structured hours	Flexible hours
Employee	Employer
Salaried	Freelance, commission
Company site	Telecommuting or home-based business
Single career	Composite careers
Lifetime career	Sequential careers

Did you circle more characteristics in column 1 or in column 2? _____

Column 1 represents careers with fewer risks, higher security, and less freedom. These careers also allow for a lower level of anxiety tolerance.

Column 2 represents careers with more risks, lower security, and more freedom. Careers like these usually call for fairly high anxiety tolerance.

Do your choices feel right for you?	**Yes**	**No**	**Undecided**
Do you consider yourself a risk taker?	**Yes**	**No**	**Undecided**
Do you often worry about future events or situations?	**Yes**	**No**	**Undecided**

Refer to this chart as you make your career decisions and explore different job titles. Would you be more comfortable in a job offering security or one providing more freedom? While these characteristics are at opposite ends of the scale, one is not better than the other. It's entirely a matter of what feels right for you.

Employee or Employer?

Another consideration, also based on your personality, is whether you would find it more rewarding to be an *employer* or an *employee*. Employers, as they relate to the following exercise, are defined as people who own their business, whatever its size. In other words, these people are *entrepreneurs*. They usually have more freedom and control over their time. However, they may often need to take major risks, both personal and financial. Is this an option that appeals to you?

ENTREPRENEURIAL CHECKLIST

Select the answer that best describes, or comes closest to, your feelings.

Willing to risk capital:

☐ 1. As long as I feel that there is a good chance of success, I'll go for it.

☐ 2. I'm willing to invest some capital, but I always want to leave a sizable cushion, just in case.

☐ 3. I have never really felt comfortable risking money or time on things I'm not absolutely sure of.

Independence:

☐ 1. Most of all, I want to be my own boss; it's my major goal.

☐ 2. I don't mind working for other people, but I'd rather be on my own.

☐ 3. Being on my own really scares me. I'd rather have the security of being an employee, and let someone else worry about the problems.

Flexibility:

☐ 1. I adapt to change quickly and decisively.

☐ 2. I move, but it takes time and careful consideration.

☐ 3. I would rather see things stay the same; I get uptight when change occurs.

Self-confidence:

☐ 1. I am very confident in myself and know that I can handle most situations.

☐ 2. I am confident most of the time, particularly when I know the ground rules.

☐ 3. I'm not in control of my destiny; other people really control my future.

Attitude toward people:

☐ 1. I am naturally drawn to people; I like them, and they like me.

☐ 2. I find most people enjoyable, and most people are attracted to me.

☐ 3. I like things more than people and don't have many friends.

Knowledge of the particular business:

☐ 1. I know the business that I've been thinking about well and will enjoy it.

☐ 2. I'm reasonably confident I can learn the business, and it appears that I will enjoy it.

☐ 3. I am not familiar with this type of business, nor do I know whether I will enjoy it.

Ability to start from scratch:

☐ 1. I enjoy the challenge of building something from scratch on my own; I'm a self-starter.

☐ 2. If given basic guidelines, I can do a good job.

☐ 3. I really prefer to have the entire job laid out, then I'll do it well.

Commitment:

- ☐ 1. I have a high drive and commitment and won't stop until the project is done.
- ☐ 2. I seem to have a higher level of perseverance when things are going well.
- ☐ 3. I start many projects, but rarely find time to finish them.

Common sense:

- ☐ 1. I consider myself realistic and "street wise" when it comes to business.
- ☐ 2. Most business situations make sense, but there are areas where I feel out of step.
- ☐ 3. I am inexperienced and impractical in business matters.

Willingness to accept failure:

- ☐ 1. "Nothing ventured, nothing gained" is my motto.
- ☐ 2. I want to succeed, but if I fail, I will accept it.
- ☐ 3. I want to avoid failure, and won't take a risk if it doesn't look like a sure thing.

Health:

- ☐ 1. I have excellent health and feel good, both physically and mentally.
- ☐ 2. I get sick on occasion, but it doesn't last long.
- ☐ 3. I have problems with my health; illness always seems to get in my way.

Work habits:

- ☐ 1. I plan before I start and then work my plan; I'm well-organized.
- ☐ 2. I find that I'm organized most of the time; but on occasion, I do get out of control.
- ☐ 3. I take things as they come, and sometimes get priorities confused.

To total your score, add up all the checked numbers. A number one has the weight of one, a number two scores a two, and a three equals three. If your total score is between 12 and 16, you are a good candidate and should consider starting your own business at some time.

Reprinted with permission: *How to Start, Expand and Sell a Business, a Complete Guidebook for Entrepreneurs* by James C. Comiskey.

What About Status?

What does status mean to you? Whose opinions matter to you most? What values does status reflect? Can you explain why, today, a rock star has more status than a teacher or a politician? Consider these questions and then, to help clarify your thoughts, indicate whether you agree or disagree with the following statements.

It is important to me to have a job with high status.

Agree   Disagree

I am willing to invest the time it takes to train for a job with high status.

Agree   Disagree

It is more important to me that a job has status than that it pays well.

Agree   Disagree

I don't think I could be happy at a job that others might look down on.

Agree   Disagree

Chapter 6

Vocabulary of Success

artistic _____

accommodate _____

protective _____

humanitarian _____

occupation _____

tentative _____

excursion _____

attributes _____

visualization _____

typical _____

mesh _____

consult _____

accurate _____

explicit _____

decisive _____

gregarious _____

contagious _____

patient _____

conscientious _____

prominent _____

Career Clusters

Review the Career Clusters (in bold), and place a check mark in the box next to those areas that sound interesting to you.

- ☐ *Agriculture, Food, and Natural Resources*
- ☐ *Architecture and Construction*
- ☐ *Arts, Audio/Video Technology, and Communications*
- ☐ *Business, Management, and Administration*
- ☐ *Education and Training*
- ☐ *Finance*
- ☐ *Government and Public Administration*
- ☐ *Health Science*

- ☐ *Hospitality and Tourism*
- ☐ *Human Services*
- ☐ *Information Technology*
- ☐ *Law, Public Safety, Corrections and Security*
- ☐ *Manufacturing*
- ☐ *Marketing, Sales, and Service*
- ☐ *Science, Technology, Engineering, and Mathematics*
- ☐ *Transportation, Distribution, and Logistics*

Which two groups sound the most appealing to you? Write them below.

_____   _____

Bring In Your Identity

The occupational groups known as career clusters are based on broad industries with commonalities such as interests, values, and skill sets. Turn back to your personal profile chart on page 27 to review your values and passions. Now go over the groups again. Below, list a couple of careers that appeal to you most, or that seem to complement your values and passions.

_____   _____   _____

_____   _____   _____

Next take another look at your strengths and skills. Do you see (or can you think of) any careers within your chosen interest group(s) that also seem to fit in with these aspects of your personality? List other possible careers on the following lines.

_____   _____   _____

_____   _____   _____

My
10yearPlan
.com

Career Interest Survey

Now it's time to choose three careers that appeal to you most and begin learning as much about them as you can. Review the careers chosen on page 147. It will be helpful if you can interview people now working in these fields as well. Separate worksheets are provided for each job.

JOB TITLE _____

1. What specific tasks would I perform on this job? (For example, a salesclerk would answer questions, tidy displays, unpack merchandise, ring up sales, make change, and so on.)

   _____

   _____

2. What is the job environment likely to be? Is this compatible with the setting I said I wanted on *page 126?*

   _____

   _____

3. What would be the rewards of working at this job? Are they the same as the ones I listed on *page 129?*

   _____

   _____

4. I would find this job particularly satisfying because: (Review your passions, values, interests, and life goals for guidance.) *See page 27.*

   _____

   _____

5. Is this job compatible with my work behavioral style? If so, in what ways? *Review pages 38–43.*

   _____

   _____

6. How much training or education would I need? Review your options (college, technical school, apprenticeship, work experience, etc.). *See pages 268–269.* What commitment am I willing to make? *Review pages 114–120.*

   _____

   _____

7. Does this job require specific physical attributes or abilities (strength or health requirements, 20/20 vision, and so on)? If so, what are they? Do I meet them?

   _____

   _____

8. What could I expect to earn as a beginner in this field? _____

What is the average mid-career salary? _____

9. Does this meet my salary requirements? *See pages 93 and 131.*   Yes   No

_____

10. Will there be many job openings when I am ready to go to work? How might societal, economic, and technological changes impact this career? *Online resources will be helpful.*

_____

_____

11. What aptitudes, strengths, and skills does this job call for? Are they transferable to another career if I change my mind or this job title becomes obsolete? *See page 132.*

_____

_____

12. What can I do today to begin preparing for this job?

_____

_____

13. What classes must I take in high school to qualify for this job?

_____

_____

14. Where in this town or state could I find a job in this field?

_____

_____

15. How does this career mesh with my family plans? Is it consistent with my desired lifestyle? *See page 130.* Does it offer opportunities for flexible hours or part-time work? Is the income high enough so I could maintain my family on it alone if necessary? Could I afford the kind of day care I'd like for my children?

_____

_____

_____

16. Are there opportunities for self-employment in this field (business owner, freelance work, consulting, and the like)?

_____

_____

Create a timeline outlining how this career has changed over the last 10 years and predicting how it might change in the next 10 years. *Start with online resources.*

JOB TITLE _____

1. What specific tasks would I perform on this job? (For example, a salesclerk would answer questions, tidy displays, unpack merchandise, ring up sales, make change, and so on.)

_____

_____

2. What is the job environment likely to be? Is this compatible with the setting I said I wanted on *page 126?*

_____

_____

3. What would be the rewards of working at this job? Are they the same as the ones I listed on *page 129?*

_____

_____

4. I would find this job particularly satisfying because: (Review your passions, values, interests, and life goals for guidance.) *See page 27.*

_____

_____

5. Is this job compatible with my work behavioral style? If so, in what ways? *Review pages 38–43.*

_____

_____

6. How much training or education would I need? Review your options (college, technical school, apprenticeship, work experience, etc.). *See pages 268–269.* What commitment am I willing to make? *Review pages 114–120.*

_____

_____

7. Does this job require specific physical attributes or abilities (strength or health requirements, 20/20 vision, and so on)? If so, what are they? Do I meet them?

_____

_____

8. What could I expect to earn as a beginner in this field? _____

   What is the average mid-career salary? _____

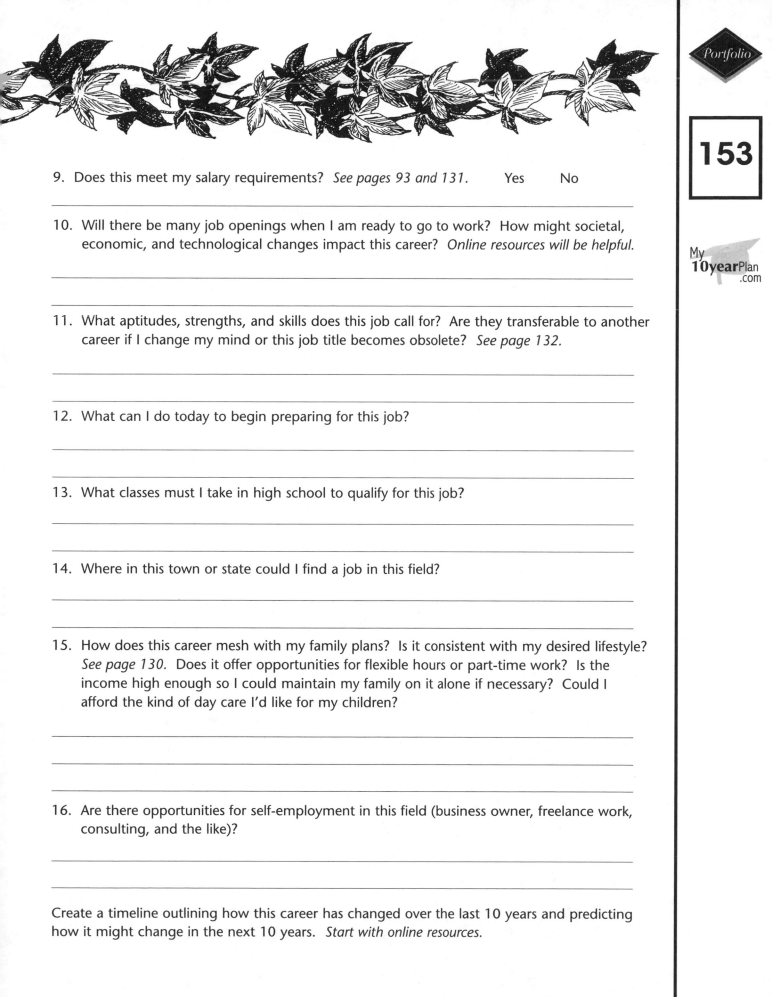

9. Does this meet my salary requirements? *See pages 93 and 131.*   Yes   No

_____

10. Will there be many job openings when I am ready to go to work? How might societal, economic, and technological changes impact this career? *Online resources will be helpful.*

_____

11. What aptitudes, strengths, and skills does this job call for? Are they transferable to another career if I change my mind or this job title becomes obsolete? *See page 132.*

_____

_____

12. What can I do today to begin preparing for this job?

_____

_____

13. What classes must I take in high school to qualify for this job?

_____

_____

14. Where in this town or state could I find a job in this field?

_____

_____

15. How does this career mesh with my family plans? Is it consistent with my desired lifestyle? *See page 130.* Does it offer opportunities for flexible hours or part-time work? Is the income high enough so I could maintain my family on it alone if necessary? Could I afford the kind of day care I'd like for my children?

_____

_____

_____

16. Are there opportunities for self-employment in this field (business owner, freelance work, consulting, and the like)?

_____

_____

Create a timeline outlining how this career has changed over the last 10 years and predicting how it might change in the next 10 years. *Start with online resources.*

JOB TITLE _____

1. What specific tasks would I perform on this job? (For example, a salesclerk would answer
    questions, tidy displays, unpack merchandise, ring up sales, make change, and so on.)

    _____

    _____

2. What is the job environment likely to be? Is this compatible with the setting I said I wanted
    on *page 126?*

    _____

    _____

3. What would be the rewards of working at this job? Are they the same as the ones I listed
    on *page 129?*

    _____

    _____

4. I would find this job particularly satisfying because: (Review your passions, values, interests,
    and life goals for guidance.) *See page 27.*

    _____

    _____

5. Is this job compatible with my work behavioral style? If so, in what ways?
    Review pages 38–43.

    _____

    _____

6. How much training or education would I need? Review your options (college, technical
    school, apprenticeship, work experience, etc.). *See pages 268–269.* What commitment
    am I willing to make? *Review pages 114–120.*

    _____

    _____

7. Does this job require specific physical attributes or abilities (strength or health requirements,
    20/20 vision, and so on)? If so, what are they? Do I meet them?

    _____

    _____

8. What could I expect to earn as a beginner in this field? _____

    What is the average mid-career salary? _____

9. Does this meet my salary requirements? *See pages 93 and 131.*   Yes   No

    _____

10. Will there be many job openings when I am ready to go to work? How might societal, economic, and technological changes impact this career? *Online resources will be helpful.*

_____

_____

11. What aptitudes, strengths, and skills does this job call for? Are they transferable to another career if I change my mind or this job title becomes obsolete? *See page 132.*

_____

_____

12. What can I do today to begin preparing for this job?

_____

_____

13. What classes must I take in high school to qualify for this job?

_____

_____

14. Where in this town or state could I find a job in this field?

_____

_____

15. How does this career mesh with my family plans? Is it consistent with my desired lifestyle? *See page 130.* Does it offer opportunities for flexible hours or part-time work? Is the income high enough so I could maintain my family on it alone if necessary? Could I afford the kind of day care I'd like for my children?

_____

_____

_____

16. Are there opportunities for self-employment in this field (business owner, freelance work, consulting, and the like)?

_____

_____

Create a timeline outlining how this career has changed over the last 10 years and predicting how it might change in the next 10 years. *Start with online resources.*

STEP TWO

SEEING IN THE MIND'S EYE

Picture yourself on the job. What would a typical working day be like? Use the information you gathered in step one to answer the following questions. Sit down, close your eyes, and actually see yourself going through the day. Pay particular attention to your feelings. Concern yourself with more than just the work. How would you feel in the morning, as you got ready to leave home? What would you do at lunch? How would you feel at the end of the day? How would you spend your evening?

IMAGING A TYPICAL DAY

If your working hours would be something other than 9:00 A.M. to 5:00 P.M., adjust the following schedule accordingly.

7:00 A.M. Getting ready for work. What would you wear? How do you feel about going to work? Are you looking forward to the day? _____

_____

8:00 A.M. Traveling to work. How would you get there? How far would you travel? Would you work at home? _____

_____

9:00 A.M. Walking into work. Describe the setting. Who else is there? What kind of greeting do you get from them? _____

_____

9:00 A.M. to 12:00 noon What would you be doing during this time? If this is a typical day, what tasks and responsibilities would you carry out?

_____

10:00 A.M. _____

11:00 A.M. _____

Noon. Where would you have lunch, and with whom? Would you socialize with co-workers? Clients?

_____

_____

1:00 P.M. to 5:00 P.M. As the day goes on, see yourself handling some special problems or challenges that might arise in this field. What are they? How do you deal with them?

_____

1:00 P.M. _____

2:00 P.M. _____

3:00 P.M. _____

4:00 P.M. _____

5:00 P.M. _____

6:00 P.M. Going home. How do you feel at the end of the day? What might you be thinking about? _____

_____

7:00 P.M. and on. How would you spend a typical evening? Would you need to bring work home? Would you be with your family? Your friends? Are there hobbies or volunteer activities you would want to pursue?

_____

_____

The Shadow Program

Write a business letter to the person of your choice, explaining what you want to do:

STEP THREE

INVOLVE ME AND I UNDERSTAND

Practice your skill at recognizing entry-level jobs by thinking of possible positions for people interested in the following careers. In column A, list jobs that will expose you to the work of each career.

Example: Mechanic = gas jockey, auto parts sales or cashier

CAREER	COLUMN A PAID	COLUMN B VOLUNTEER
Attorney		
Social Worker		
Accountant		
Veterinarian		
Police Officer		
Retail Salesperson		
Classical Musician		
Politician		
Hairstylist		
Office Manager		

HINT: If all else fails, most businesses will allow you to come in for a few hours each week and run errands. Author Mindy Bingham's brother did this for a law firm while he was in high school; he owns that same law firm today.

From your paid or volunteer work
CRITIQUE YOUR EXPERIENCE

Do you like the setting?	Yes	No
Is what is happening exciting?	Yes	No
Does the pace of the day match your personality?	Yes	No
Is the level of responsibility comfortable?	Yes	No
Is the level of responsibility threatening?	Yes	No
Does the work hold your interest?	Yes	No
Could this become boring after a short time?	Yes	No
Do you like the people you work with?	Yes	No

How do your co-workers feel about their jobs? Write your observations here:

_____

_____

TEAM BUILDING

Match the four people described below with the job for which his or her chemistry test would "qualify" them in each of the work environments listed. If you were in charge of the businesses, how would you assign these employees to build the most effective team?

Ellen's preferred behavior style is dominance. She is a high-energy individual who likes to be in charge of what she is doing. She is decisive and always looks for the most efficient way to do things. She likes to solve problems, is comfortable with change, and is very goal directed.

Robert's style is influencing. He is a creative person who likes flexibility in his work environment. He is gregarious and likes to work with people. Robert's enthusiasm can be contagious. He is good at persuading people to act. He likes varied tasks and will take calculated risks.

Michiko is most comfortable with steadiness. She likes to work with other people, particularly in a supportive role. A patient and considerate person, Michiko likes tasks with well-defined procedures. A steady worker, she follows her project through from beginning to end. She is a listener and a doer.

Romero's preferred style is compliance. He is extremely detail oriented and is likely to question the decisions of others. He wants to know the facts behind the issues. A conscientious worker, he is precise in any task he undertakes and wants to make sure it is done accurately.

MATCHING WORK STYLES TO JOBS

How would you assign the jobs below to these four individuals?

BOOK PUBLISHING EXAMPLE
Publisher: *Ellen*
Sales Rep: *Robert*
Book designer: *Michiko*
Editor: *Romero*

CONSTRUCTION

Draftsperson _____

Contractor _____

Architect _____

Carpenter _____

HOSPITAL

Minister/priest/rabbi _____

Administrator _____

Lab technician _____

Physician _____

FACTORY

Cafeteria chef _____

Assembly line worker _____

Foreman _____

Quality control inspector _____

SCHOOL

Secretary _____

Principal _____

Attendance clerk _____

Counselor _____

BANK

Loan officer _____

Bank teller _____

Manager _____

Accountant _____

RESEARCH LAB

Project manager _____

Fundraiser _____

Scientist _____

Computer programmer _____

Can you identify which personality type would likely be happiest in each of the jobs below?

PHYSICIAN

Anesthesiologist _____

Surgeon _____

Chief of physicians at local hospital _____

Teacher at medical school _____

TEACHER

Teacher in public school system _____

Private tutor or coach _____

Professor of accounting at university level _____

Trainer for major corporation _____

CHEF

Head chef in a large restaurant—tastes everything! _____

Catering company owner _____

Teacher of adult education cooking classes _____

Associate chef in a restaurant _____

Which career seems to be your favorite choice at this point in time? What work behavior style do you think would be prominent in someone happy with this job?

_____

Why? _____

_____

Does this match your personal work style? Review your answers on page 42.

Yes   No   Perhaps

In what ways?

_____

_____

Information on personality styles is adapted from the widely-used DiSC™ Dimensions of Behavior model and the *Personal Profile System*® assessment instrument, ™copyright 1972, Carlson Learning Company. Used with permission of Carlson Learning Company, Minneapolis, Minnesota.

Chapter 7

Vocabulary of Success

alma mater _____

automatic _____

issue _____

logical _____

evaluate _____

differentiate _____

essential _____

gratification _____

long-term _____

pro _____

con _____

probability _____

analyze _____

apprenticeship _____

certification _____

expedite _____

agonize _____

fret _____

avoidance _____

tendency _____

Identifying Choices

List Joyce's goals below.

1. _____

2. _____

Which would you say is her long-term goal? Which is her short-term goal?

What is Joyce's long-term goal? _____

What are the options she must choose from now that will effect her long-term goal?

1. _____

2. _____

3. _____

Gathering Information

Can you list some other information that would be helpful to Joyce as she weighs her alternatives?

1. _____

2. _____

3. _____

4. _____

Evaluating Choices

On the chart below, evaluate Joyce's other choice—not to work at all so she can concentrate on her studies.

Identify your choices	Evaluate your choices		
	Pros	Cons	Probability of success
Not work at all	_____ _____	_____ _____	_____ _____

JESSICA'S STORY

Use the chart below to identify Jessica's choices and evaluate each one.

Identify your choices	Evaluate your choices		
	Pros	Cons	Probability of success
1. _____ _____	_____ _____	_____ _____	_____ _____
2. _____ _____	_____ _____	_____ _____	_____ _____
3. _____ _____	_____ _____	_____ _____	_____ _____
4. _____ _____	_____ _____	_____ _____	_____ _____

If you were Jessica, what would you do? _____

_____

_____

JOHN'S STORY

Use the chart below to identify John's choices and evaluate each one.

Identify your choices	Evaluate your choices		
	Pros	Cons	Probability of success
1. _____ _____	_____ _____	_____ _____	_____ _____
2. _____ _____	_____ _____	_____ _____	_____ _____
3. _____ _____	_____ _____	_____ _____	_____ _____
4. _____ _____	_____ _____	_____ _____	_____ _____

If you were John, what would you do? _____

_____

_____

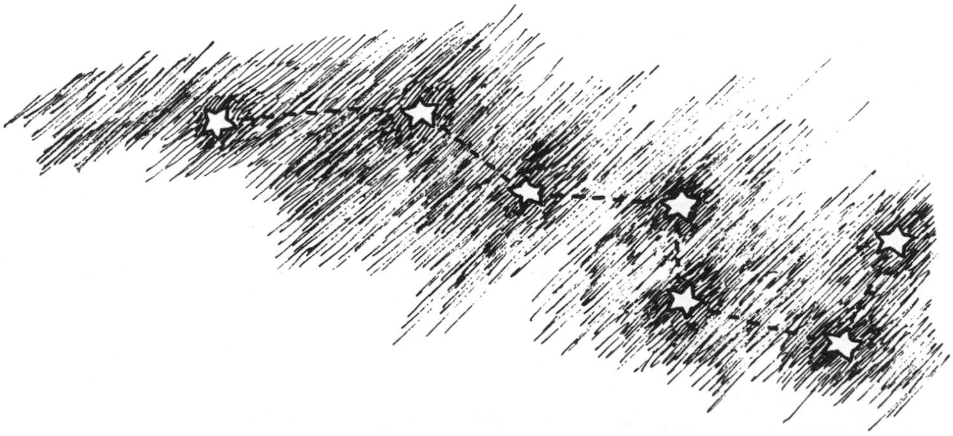

GLORIA'S CHART

What choice would you make if you were Gloria? _____

_____

DECISON-MAKING RUBRIC

Complete the chart below for yourself. Identify and evaluate four possible career choices.

Goal: To identify a career that I will find satisfying.

Decision to be made: Which career would I find most satisfying?

My resources: _____

_____

_____

_____

My wants and needs: _____

_____

_____

_____

Gather information: _____

Identify your choices	Evaluate your choices		
	Pros	Cons	Probability of success
1. _____ _____	_____ _____	_____ _____	_____ _____
2. _____ _____	_____ _____	_____ _____	_____ _____
3. _____ _____	_____ _____	_____ _____	_____ _____
4. _____ _____	_____ _____	_____ _____	_____ _____

Make a choice _____

How realistic is this choice? _____

Make a Decision

What is your decision-making (or avoiding) style? Check the places along the scale below that you think best represent your personality. If the words in the left-hand column describe your behavior, you may tend to avoid making decisions. On the other hand, if your behavior is better described by the words on the right, you may tend to make decisions too quickly. There is no right or wrong spot on the scale. But, by being aware of your tendencies, you may be better able to use them in your best interest.

passive	_____ _____ _____ _____ _____ _____ _____	aggressive
contemplative	_____ _____ _____ _____ _____ _____ _____	impulsive
controlled	_____ _____ _____ _____ _____ _____ _____	free
rational	_____ _____ _____ _____ _____ _____ _____	emotional
easily influenced	_____ _____ _____ _____ _____ _____ _____	self-directed
delaying	_____ _____ _____ _____ _____ _____ _____	expediting
cautious	_____ _____ _____ _____ _____ _____ _____	risk-taking
structured	_____ _____ _____ _____ _____ _____ _____	creative
agonizing	_____ _____ _____ _____ _____ _____ _____	relaxed

Chapter 8

Vocabulary of Success

opportunities _____

flatter _____

courage _____

reputation _____

motivation _____

technique _____

temporary _____

abstract _____

postpone _____

struggle _____

joyous _____

temptation _____

wishful _____

privy _____

discipline _____

destructive _____

goal _____

objective _____

diagram _____

beliefs _____

SOLVING PROBLEMS

Who is responsible for solving Crystal and Sterling's problem?

_____

If they get married right away, what sacrifices might they have to make?

_____

_____

If they wait and get married when they graduate from college, what sacrifices will they

have to make? _____

_____

What facts should Crystal and Sterling consider before they make their decision?

_____

_____

What wishful thinking might come into play as they make their decision? How likely is

that to happen? _____

If you were Sterling and Crystal, what would you do? _____

_____

Setting Goals and Objectives

Diagram Marta's objectives:

Goal: To answer my questions about archaeology by March 1.

Objective 1: Read at least one book or four articles on archaeology by January 20.

Objective 2: Search the Internet for information and discussion groups by January 25.

Objective 3A: Call City College and the Natural History Museum by January 31
to see if there are any archaelologists on staff.

Objective 3B: If so, interview a working archaeologist by February 14.

Objective 4: Research climate and reptile life at the three most appealing field sites
by February 21.

Now write and diagram some objectives of your own.

To buy a new car in six months.

To save for a trip to _____ after graduation.

To make the _____ team next year.

To earn an A in _____ class.

To be accepted at _____ after high school graduation.
(school)

Goal: _____

    Objectives:

      1. _____

      2. _____

      3. _____

Goal: _____

    Objectives:

      1. _____

      2. _____

      3. _____

YOUR LIFESTYLE GOALS

Now write lifestyle goals and objectives of your own.

Your lifestyle goal: _____

    Objectives:

      1. _____

      2. _____

      3. _____

Your lifestyle goal: _____

    Objectives:

      1. _____

      2. _____

      3. _____

Your lifestyle goal: _____

    Objectives:

      1. _____

      2. _____

      3. _____

My
10yearPlan
.com

Chapter 9

Vocabulary of Success

detour _____

challenge _____

ironic _____

affliction _____

paraplegic _____

debilitate _____

orator _____

serenity _____

solution _____

median _____

consideration _____

obligation _____

valedictorian _____

ambition _____

evidence _____

obstacle _____

concentration _____

confront _____

confident _____

progressive _____

What's Your Excuse?

- ☐ I'm a woman
- ☐ I'm a man
- ☐ I'm black
- ☐ I'm white
- ☐ I'm Hispanic
- ☐ I'm Asian
- ☐ I come from a different culture
- ☐ I'm rich
- ☐ I'm poor
- ☐ I'm too smart
- ☐ I'm not smart enough
- ☐ I'm too ugly
- ☐ I'm too fat
- ☐ I'm too thin
- ☐ I'm too short
- ☐ I'm too tall
- ☐ I'm blind
- ☐ I have impaired vision
- ☐ I'm deaf
- ☐ I have a hearing loss
- ☐ I can't speak
- ☐ I have a speech impediment
- ☐ I'm a paraplegic

- ☐ I'm a quadriplegic
- ☐ I'm physically disfigured
- ☐ I've lost a limb
- ☐ I have a debilitating disease
- ☐ I've been treated for emotional problems
- ☐ I've been persecuted for my beliefs
- ☐ I've had a serious illness
- ☐ I'm shy
- ☐ I'm adopted
- ☐ I'm an orphan
- ☐ I come from a single-parent home
- ☐ I've been abused
- ☐ I've been in trouble with the law
- ☐ I'm chemically dependent
- ☐ I'm homeless
- ☐ I have to take care of a parent or sibling
- ☐ I have a baby
- ☐ My family won't let me
- ☐ My family expects too much of me
- ☐ No one believes in me
- ☐ People have convinced me I can't
- ☐ I can't do it because...
- ☐ Other _____

Do you know of any people in your own community who have overcome handicaps or adversities in their lives? If so, add their names below. These people are all heroes, and they can be inspiring role models.

_____

_____

Taking Responsibility

Can you think of any excuses you've made recently that made it seem something or someone else was responsible for your predicament? Write them below.

1. _____

2. _____

3. _____

Now analyze your own role in those situations and rewrite the statements, this time taking responsibility for the problem.

1. _____

2. _____

3. _____

STARTLING STATEMENT QUIZ

Circle the answer you think most accurately completes each of the following statements.

1. Each year _____ women under 20 in the United States become pregnant.
    a. 250,000
    b. 500,000
    c. 750,000
    d. 1 million

2. _____ percent of teen mothers graduate or earn a GED by the time they are 22 years old.
    a. 34
    b. 51
    c. 66
    d. 85

3. In 2009, _____ percent of families headed by a female lived in poverty.
    a. 12.7
    b. 21.6
    c. 29.9
    d. 40.9

4. In March 2011, the overall unemployment rate was 8.9 percent. For high school dropouts, the rate was _____ percent.
    a. 5.7
    b. 11.3
    c. 16.2
    d. 20.5

5. In 2009, _____ percent of blacks that did not complete high school lived in poverty. For those who completed college, the poverty rate was only 3.2 percent.
    a. 9.7
    b. 14.8
    c. 19.6
    d. 26.7

6. In 2009, _____ percent of 18- to 24-year-olds had left high school without a diploma.
    a. 2
    b. 9
    c. 13
    d. 20

7. In 2009, the median income for full-time workers 25 years and over with a bachelor's degree or more was $51,878 for women and $71,466 for men. The median income for workers with no high school diploma was _____ for women and _____ for men.
    a. $14,387 and $20,526
    b. $21,226 and $28,023
    c. $24,903 and $31,632
    d. $33,546 and $38,748

8. Teens that start drinking before the age of 14 are nearly _____ times more likely than adults that start drinking after they turn 21 to eventually become alcoholics.
    a. 3
    b. 4
    c. 6
    d. 7

9. _____ percent of the 33,808 total traffic fatalities in 2009 were caused by alcohol-related crashes.
    a. 14
    b. 23
    c. 32
    d. 41

10. The leading cause of death for 15- to 20-year-olds is motor vehicle crashes. In 2009, _____ percent of 15- to 20-year-old drivers who were killed in crashes were intoxicated.
    a. 7
    b. 15
    c. 24
    d. 32

11. While the use of many illicit drugs has dropped, abuse of marijuana is rising. In 2009, _____ percent of high school seniors reported using marijuana within the past month.
    a. 4.7
    b. 10.9
    c. 16.1
    d. 20.6

No portion of this book may be photocopied or reproduced electronically without written permission from the publisher.

91

Dana and Miko

Who acted impulsively? In what way? _____

_____

Try to imagine what the future holds for Dana and Miko. Describe their lives 15 years later in the space below.

Dana's life: _____

_____

_____

Miko's life: _____

_____

_____

Josie and Juan — Judy and Joe

Which couple acted impulsively? In what way? _____

_____

_____

What could life be like for these two couples in 15 years? Visualize their futures and describe them below.

Josie and Juan's life: _____

_____

_____

_____

Judy and Joe's life: _____

_____

_____

_____

_____

204

205

Sam and Janice

Who acted impulsively? In what way? _____

_____

Describe what you think Sam and Janice's lives might be like 15 years from now.

Sam's life: _____

_____

_____

_____

_____

Janice's life: _____

_____

_____

_____

_____

Is It Worth Staying in School?

You decide. Go back to pages 150–151. What careers did you say you might like? List them below.

_____

Imagine that you quit school before graduation. Could you qualify for any of these jobs without a high school diploma?

Yes   **No**

If so, which ones? _____

If not, you need another plan. Review the Your Personal Profile chart on page 27, your preferred lifestyle on page 63, your budget requirements on page 93 or your hardship budget on page 96, and your career portrait and priorities on page 134.

Now go through the career search process on pages 150–151 once more. This time, though, make sure that a high school diploma isn't required for the jobs you are investigating.

List three careers that meet your personal requirements but do not require a high school diploma below.

_____

Compare these jobs with the ones you listed at the top of the page. How are they different? Which careers do you think would be more satisfying? Why?

_____

_____

_____

_____

Imagine your life 15 years from now. What do you think it would be like if you take a job from your second list, the one that doesn't require a high school education? Which would you find more satisfying—a career from the first or second list?

_____

_____

_____

The Economics of Bad Habits

Complete the chart below:

	One pack/day	Other use for money
Cost/year	$	
Cost/10 years	$	
Cost/60 years	$	

Some habits are much more expensive than cigarettes. Before you get involved with them, use the same equation to determine how much they would cost you over a lifetime.

Habit _____

Cost/day _____   Cost/week _____

		Other use for money
Cost/year	$	
Cost/10 years	$	
Cost/60 years	$	

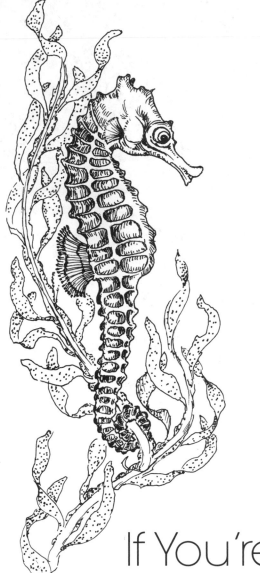

If You're A Woman

Let's explore this concept further. Do you think the workers in each of the careers below are mostly men or mostly women? In the first column beside each job title, write an F if you believe more females work in this field, an M if you think more men do.

Now go back and circle the careers that would probably offer the most flexible hours. In other words, which workers could most easily decide to take time off in the afternoon to attend a son or daughter's basketball game? Some careers are decidedly more flexible than others.

_____	Child care worker	_____	Architect
_____	Office clerks, general	_____	Auto body repairer
_____	Cashier	_____	Chemical engineer
_____	Janitor	_____	Computer programmer
_____	Nurse (RN)	_____	Air traffic controller
_____	Plumber	_____	Securities sales rep
_____	Elementary school teacher	_____	Chiropractor (self employed)

Child care worker	$18,605	Architect	$70,320
Office clerks, general	$25,320	Auto body repairer	$36,332
Cashier	$17,320	Chemical engineer	$74,600
Janitor	$21,032	Computer programmer	$69,620
Nurse (RN)	$62,450	Air traffic controller	$111,870
Plumber	$44,758	Securities sales representative	$68,680
Elementary school teacher	$47,100	Chiropractor (self-employed)	$94,454

Source: U.S. Department of Labor, Bureau of Labor Statistics, *Occupational Outlook Handbook*, 2010–2011 Edition.

Along the bottom of the following graph, first list the careers that are held mostly by women, beginning on the left-hand bottom column. We've already included the child care worker and office clerk as examples. Next add the jobs held mostly by men. Now, star the flexible careers, jobs in which workers can choose their own hours. We've used the chiropractor as an example.

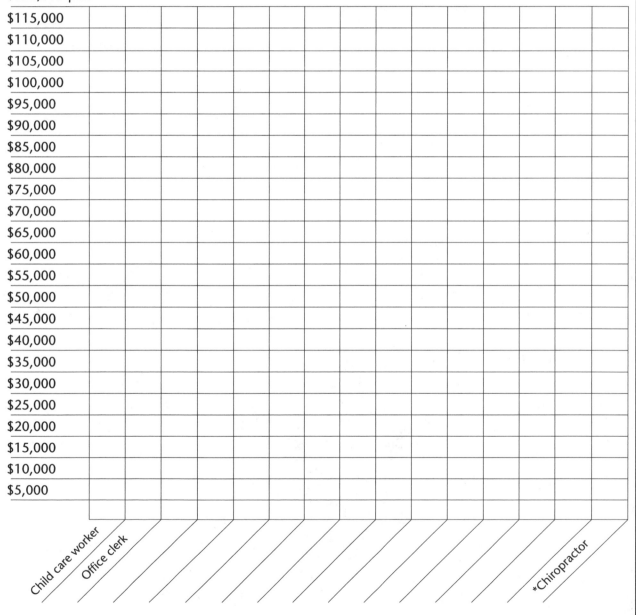

NOTE: Because we try to maintain current salary figures, the numbers in your workbook may not match the numbers in your textbook. Consider the workbook figures current.

Now use a pencil to chart the annual average salaries of the flexible careers. Use a pen to chart the annual average salaries of the non-flexible careers. (Note: The salaries we've used come from Department of Labor sources. Individuals might be able to earn a higher salary by working freelance or starting their own small businesses.)

Suppose a woman with three children suddenly found herself the sole support of her family. Decide what a family this size in your community needs a year to live in minimal comfort.

$ _____ per year

Now, draw a double line across the chart at this dollar level.

Which careers from the list would be most suitable for parenting? That is, which would provide both flexibility and an adequate salary? List those careers below. (Hint: These careers are graphed in pencil, above the double line.)

_____

_____

Which of the careers on your list require either a college or vocational degree or some other type of special training? Circle them.

Do more men or women currently hold these jobs?

More men   More women

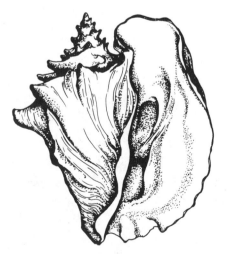

BEFORE YOU GIVE UP

Can you think of a dream or ambition you had in the past that you have abandoned? Something you wanted to do or accomplish? Perhaps you dreamed of singing a solo in the school concert or asking your neighbor to the Spring dance. Maybe, while watching *Law & Order* you've dreamed of becoming an attorney.

Think of a dream that you have given up or are considering giving up? (If you haven't given your dreams much thought, now is the time to start thinking about them seriously. Try to write them down when they come to mind.)

Before you decide to give up something you once thought you wanted badly, answer the following questions.

What was your old dream? _____

How long did you hold it? _____

When did you decide to give up your dream? _____

Why? _____

What is your new dream? _____

Why does it appeal to you now? _____

Is there hard evidence to support your decision to give up your dream (you can't carry a tune, you've flunked out of school, you've run out of money, etc.)?

_____

If so, is this just an obstacle, or have you really reached the end of the road?

_____

If there is no hard evidence, have you discussed your decision with your teachers or your advisor? What do they think?

_____

If you've come up against an obstacle, would you hang on to your dream if the obstacle would simply disappear (the math requirement is lifted, you win the sweepstakes)?

_____

If you've decided to give up your dream because of some rational obstacle (money, grades), think of as many possible ways to overcome your problem as you can. List them below. Are any of them workable?

_____

_____

CONQUERING YOUR FEARS

Write a guided visualization below that might help you conquer a fear you currently have. Try to see yourself actually doing whatever it is that makes you anxious and write the process below.

217

_____

_____

_____

_____

_____

YOUR COURAGE ACTION PLAN

List five fears you have or situations you are avoiding.

1. _____

2. _____

3. _____

4. _____

221

5. _____

Which of these do you think would be easiest for you to overcome? Which would be hardest? List your fears again, starting with the situation that causes you the least anxiety and working toward the item that makes you feel most uncomfortable.

1. _____

2. _____

3. _____

4. _____

5. _____

Think of a plan to confront the first two items on your list. Write your plan below.

_____

_____

_____

Once you put your plans into action, record your feeling and experiences.

_____

_____

CAREER BACK-UP PLAN

Keeping your own career area of interest in mind, map out career alternatives based on the chart below. We've included Amira's chart to use as a guide along with an example for someone interested in teaching*.

1. First, write your ideal job title in the box that corresponds with the required training or education. Use a different color pen or all capital letters for that one box.

2. In the *starred* box ★, write the industry or career cluster with which this career is affiliated.

3. Based on the different commitments to education and training (column 1), choose at least one other job within that career interest area and put that job title in the corresponding box, along with the annual median salary. The *Occupational Outlook Handbook,* print or online (see page 148), will be your best resource.

ALTERNATIVE CAREER LADDER						
Education/Training Level	Job Title	Median Annual Salary	Job Title	Median Annual Salary	Job Title	Median Annual Salary
	HEALTH SERVICES		EDUCATION		★	
Doctoral or Professional Degree	**DOCTOR**	$186,044	**District Superintendent**	$159,634		
Masters Degree	**Nurse Practitioner**	$ 82,590	**School Principal**	$ 83,880		
Bachelor + Work Experience or Certification	**Medical Sonographer**	$ 61,980	**Special Ed Teacher**	$ 50,020		
Bachelor Degree	**Registered Nurse**	$ 62,450	**SCHOOL TEACHER**	$ 53,150		
Associate Degree	**Medical Assistant**	$ 28,300	**Payroll Clerk**	$ 34,810		
Postsecondary Vocational Certificate	**Medical Transcriber**	$ 32,053	**Executive Secretary**	$ 40,030		
Long-term on-the-job training	**Pharmacy Technician**	$ 27,706	**Cafeteria Cook**	$ 20,460		
Moderate-term on-the-job training	**Pharmacy Aide**	$ 20,093	**Child Care Worker**	$ 21,902		
Short-term on-the-job training	**Home Care Aide**	$ 19,178	**School Bus Driver**	$ 26,603		
No High School Diploma	**Gift Shop Cashier**	$ 17,659	**School Janitor**	$ 22,145		

* NOTE: The education and training required, as well as the median annual salary levels, will vary from state to state. These are national averages.

Write your 10-year plan for Yorik:

Year one:

Education and training: _____

Living arrangements: _____

Employment: _____

Finances: _____

Year three:

Education and training: _____

Living arrangements: _____

Employment: _____

Finances: _____

Year five:

Education and training: _____

Living arrangements: _____

Employment: _____

Finances: _____

Year eight:

Education and training: _____

Living arrangements: _____

Employment: _____

Finances: _____

Year ten:

Education and training: _____

Living arrangements: _____

Employment: _____

Finances: _____

How did Yorik delay gratification in the plan you just described? _____

_____

How might he have acted impulsively? _____

_____

Did he take responsibility for himself?   Yes   No

What excuses might a less determined person have made? _____

_____

What anxieties might he have had to overcome? _____

Chapter 10

Vocabulary of Success

attitude _____

pretend _____

affirmation _____

effective _____

reverse _____

capable _____

excellence _____

expectation _____

enthusiasm _____

prophecies _____

livelihood _____

enterprise _____

efficient _____

ethic _____

aggression _____

tardy _____

elapse _____

global _____

enormous _____

dignity _____

Affirmations

We've included a few statements as examples. Use them if they could be helpful for you. Then write your own affirmations in the space below. Repeat them to yourself often. Act as if they are true now.

231

I, _____, am confident when meeting new people.

I, _____, am capable of getting a good job.

I, _____, am good at making and keeping friends.

I, _____, am _____

I, _____, am _____

I, _____, am _____

236

Going For It . . . Work Is an Aggressive Act

How aggressive are you when you take on a job? Consider the following situations before you make up your mind.

SCENARIO 1
You are trapped in a burning house. The firefighters arrive, but the doors are locked. Would you prefer to have them

   a. wait patiently for a locksmith (the "nice" thing) or

   b. kick in the doors and windows and get you *out* of there (extremely aggressive behavior)?

SCENARIO 2
You are unjustly accused of a crime. During your trial, your lawyer uncovers evidence that proves your accuser is lying. Should your lawyer

   a. refuse to confront the witness because it wouldn't be polite or

   b. nail him to the wall?

SCENARIO 3
Your car won't start. You need to be at an important conference in an hour. When you call the repair shop, would you rather have the mechanic

   a. sympathize with your plight or

   b. be at your house within 10 minutes and have you on your way in 15?

SCENARIO 4
You are a doctor. You witness a traffic accident in which a child is seriously injured. Should you

   a. try to find out the name of the child's doctor and call him or her or

   b. do what is necessary to save the child's life?

SCENARIO 5
You are one of five junior executives in a small corporation. Each of you is asked to write a proposal for increasing sales. Should you

   a. be careful not to outdo your co-workers or

   b. do your best, for your own sake and the company's?

SCENARIO 6
You are a newspaper reporter who hears a rumor that, if true, could drastically affect the lives of many of your readers. Should you

   a. hope someone will call and tell you what's going on or

   b. investigate vigorously to either verify the story or prove it's not true?

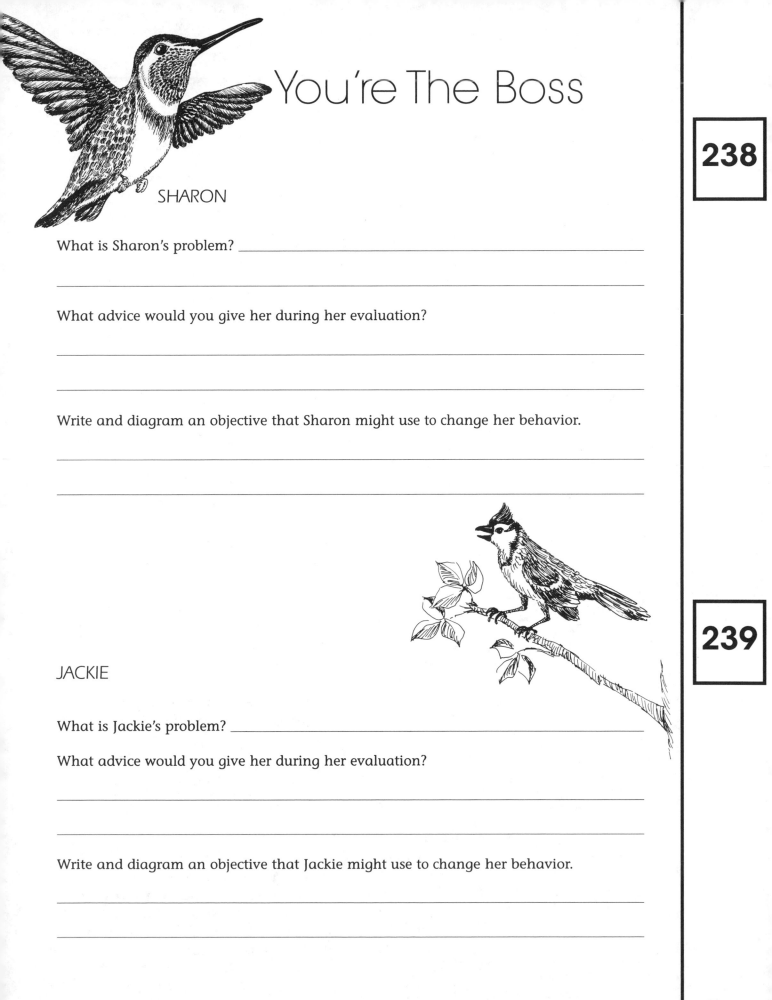

You're The Boss

SHARON

What is Sharon's problem? _____

_____

What advice would you give her during her evaluation?

_____

_____

Write and diagram an objective that Sharon might use to change her behavior.

_____

_____

JACKIE

What is Jackie's problem? _____

What advice would you give her during her evaluation?

_____

_____

Write and diagram an objective that Jackie might use to change her behavior.

_____

_____

DOROTHY

What is Dorothy's problem? _____

What advice would you give her during her evaluation?

_____

_____

Write and diagram an objective that Dorothy might use to change her behavior.

_____

_____

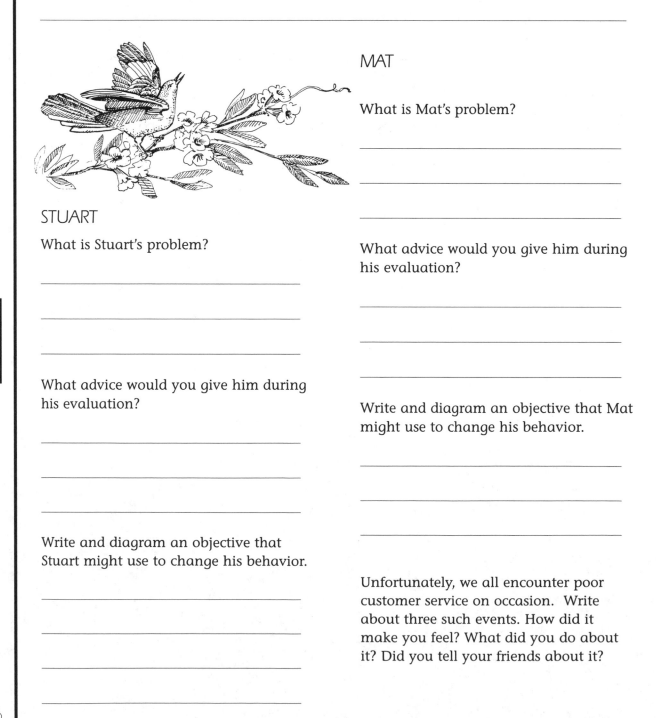

MAT

What is Mat's problem?

_____

_____

What advice would you give him during his evaluation?

_____

_____

_____

Write and diagram an objective that Mat might use to change his behavior.

_____

_____

_____

STUART

What is Stuart's problem?

_____

_____

_____

What advice would you give him during his evaluation?

_____

_____

_____

Write and diagram an objective that Stuart might use to change his behavior.

_____

_____

_____

Unfortunately, we all encounter poor customer service on occasion. Write about three such events. How did it make you feel? What did you do about it? Did you tell your friends about it?

239

240

TRAITS OF THOSE WHO GET AHEAD

Now that you've considered some less-than-perfect workers, can you describe a model employee? It might help to review the profiles above. If the characteristics described are undesirable, what opposite traits would make an employee valued by his or her employer?

Employee	Problem	Desired Behavior
Sharon	Tardiness	_____
Jackie	Untruthfulness	_____
Dorothy	Difficult Personality	_____
Stuart	Dishonesty	_____
Mat	Laziness	_____

What characteristic did Tim display in each of the situations?

_____

_____

Describe the characteristics of people you would like to hire for your business. Who do you want on your "team?"

_____

_____

Interview three local employers to find out what they expect of their employees. Ask them to rank the characteristics they look for in order of importance. Would someone with each of those characteristics, but limited work experience, still be a good job candidate? Why? How important are character traits like honesty, dependability, punctuality, respect, and getting along with co-workers?

The Employee of the Twenty-first Century

How well will you function in this new environment? The following self-evaluation quiz should give you some idea. Select the answer that best describes or comes closest to your feelings.

1. I view computers as:
   - ☐ a. an important tool.
   - ☐ b. useful at times.
   - ☐ c. . . . I don't want anything to do with them.

2. If I need to learn a new procedure while working on a computer, I:
   - ☐ a. figure it out after looking it up in the manual or online tutorial.
   - ☐ b. get help from someone who knows what to do.
   - ☐ c. give up—it takes too much time, and I didn't want to do it anyway.

3. I think of technology as:
   - ☐ a. something we all need to know and understand.
   - ☐ b. . . . I don't think about it much.
   - ☐ c. not very relevant to my life.

4. When I get my diploma at graduation, I'll probably think:
   - ☐ a. this is really just the beginning of my education.
   - ☐ b. about what I'm going to do now.
   - ☐ c. thank goodness, no more school.

5. When I have a question about something, I:
   - ☐ a. look up the answer on the Internet or call someone who should know.
   - ☐ b. make a mental note to keep my eyes open for the answer.
   - ☐ c. forget about it—it probably wasn't important anyway.

6. I think of change:
   - ☐ a. as an opportunity.
   - ☐ b. with caution.
   - ☐ c. with resistance.

7. If, halfway through a project, it becomes apparent that my plan for completing it won't work, I would:
   - ☐ a. rethink my plan and come up with a better one.
   - ☐ b. worry about the project and hope to come up with a better plan someday.
   - ☐ c. lose interest and scrap the project.

8. When I'm around people from other cultures:
   - ☐ a. I appreciate their diversity.
   - ☐ b. I'm curious—but cautious.
   - ☐ c. . . . I am uncomfortable with people who are not like me.

9. The idea of traveling to other countries:
   - ☐ a. sounds exciting to me.
   - ☐ b. is of some interest to me.
   - ☐ c. does not interest me at all.

10. Learning at least one other language:
   - ☐ a. is important for everyone.
   - ☐ b. is probably a good idea.
   - ☐ c. is unnecessary—I can get by speaking only English.

Your objectives:

Technology:

1. _____

2. _____

Love of learning:

1. _____

2. _____

Flexibility:

1. _____

2. _____

International perspective:

1. _____

2. _____

Transferable Skills Chart

Using a spreadsheet program, create your own transferable skills chart to store on the hard drive of your computer. As you acquire new skills, you can easily update this important planning document. Directions: Along the left column, keep a record of all the skills you are acquiring. As you go through school and training, update this list often. Along the top row, list all the careers that you find of interest using as many columns as you like. Then at the bottom of each column, list the skills still needed to be qualified for that particular job. Below is an abbreviated version of one high school senior's transferable skills chart.

MY SKILLS	POSSIBLE CAREERS		
	Web Designer	Real Estate Agent	Golf Pro (self-employed)
Typing 80 wpm	X	X	X
Public speaking "wizard"		X	X
Computer graphics software	X	X	
Top notch writing skills	X	X	
Bookkeeping/Accounting		X	X
Car tune ups			
Golf (3 handicap)			X
	NEEDED SKILLS:		
	Computer programming	Real estate license	Golf circuit ranking
	Web-based software	Sales technique	Marketing and promotion
	Graphic design		Small business management

My 10yearPlan .com

Chapter 11

Vocabulary of Success

principles _____

_____

publication _____

_____

resume _____

_____

summary _____

_____

original _____

_____

chronological _____

_____

honesty _____

_____

references _____

_____

draft _____

_____

polite _____

_____

impression _____

_____

vaccination _____

_____

misdemeanor _____

_____

felony _____

_____

appropriate _____

_____

rejection _____

_____

mentor _____

_____

inspirational _____

_____

tragedy _____

_____

negotiable _____

_____

Use this page to write either a draft of a resume for yourself or format one on a computer, print it, and paste it here.

Job Applications

Some forms ask for information you may not know offhand. Ask your parents for help if you don't remember any of the following:

Your mother's maiden (unmarried) name _____

Previous addresses if you've moved in recent years _____

Illnesses or health problems you've had _____

Dates of your last physical and/or vaccinations _____

Some other questions you should be prepared to answer include the following:

Do you have the legal right to work in the United States?   Yes   No
(If you are a U.S. citizen or have a work visa, answer yes.)

How will you get to and from work? _____

When are you available to work (days and hours)? _____

How many hours a week do you want to work? _____

What salary do you expect? _____

Have you served in the military?   Yes   No

Have you ever been convicted of a misdemeanor or felony?   Yes   No

Most forms ask you to sign and date your application before you turn it in to the employer. Your signature indicates that the information you have provided is true and complete. It also gives the employer the right to contact schools, former employers, or references to verify your answers.

The Job Interview

You might be asked some or all of the following questions. Write your answers here:

Why do you think you would be good at this job? _____

_____

How did you hear about this company? _____

Why do you want to work here? _____

_____

What classes are you taking in school? _____

_____

What is your favorite class? _____

What is your grade point average? _____

What are your strengths? _____

_____

What are your weaknesses? _____

_____

What are your hobbies? _____

What are your plans for the future? _____

_____

When would you be able to start working here? _____

How many hours a week could you work? _____

How would you get to and from work? _____

What salary would you need to earn? _____

Is there anything you'd like to ask me about the job? _____

_____

_____

Making Connections

Can you think of people who have served as mentors for you in the past? List them below. What did they do that you found helpful?

_____

_____

_____

How about now? Are there potential or actual mentors in your life? List them here. How have they, or how could they, help you?

_____

_____

_____

Think about the training or work you are currently planning to get or do in the next 10 years. What kinds of mentors do you need? List them by title or classification below.

_____

_____

_____

Have you ever been a mentor? To whom? What did you do? How did you feel about it?

_____

_____

_____

Chapter 12

Vocabulary of Success

overwhelming _____

alternative _____

misfortune _____

alienate _____

despotism _____

solace _____

chasten _____

virtue _____

duration _____

perspective _____

patience _____

surmount _____

muff _____

fantasies _____

impress _____

genius _____

niche _____

respect _____

appreciation _____

success _____

What Is Your Commitment to Your Education?

On page 177 you indicated the career for which you want to prepare. Write that job title in the space below.

_____

How much education and/or training will you need to complete before you can get an entry-level job in this field? If you haven't already, update your *Career Interest Survey* on pages 150–151 for this particular career?

EDUCATION or TRAINING	DURATION
_____	_____
_____	_____
_____	_____
_____	_____
	Total _____

Use the information above to determine how many more years of formal education or training you need. Enter that number below.

_____ years

What educational requirements must you meet during each of those years (classes you need to take, grades you must maintain, and so forth)? List them on the following chart. What specialized training or skills do you need? Include this information as well.

Your Education and Training 10-Year Plan

HIGH SCHOOL

This year:

_____   _____
_____   _____

Next year:

_____   _____
_____   _____

The year after:

_____   _____
_____   _____

And on . . .

_____   _____
_____   _____

POST-HIGH SCHOOL

Year one:

_____   _____
_____   _____

Year two:

_____   _____
_____   _____

Year three:

_____   _____
_____   _____

Year four:

_____   _____
_____   _____

Year five:

_____   _____
_____   _____

Year six:

_____   _____
_____   _____

Year seven:

_____   _____
_____   _____

And on . . .

LIFE-LONG LEARNING GRAPH

Lifespan Graph

Write your vision of each decade below.

90 _____

80 _____

70 _____

60 _____

50 _____

40 _____

30 _____

Write your Education and Professional Growth Plan for each of the next 10 to 15 years. You'll want to start at the bottom of the page and work your way up.

29 _____

28 _____

27 _____

26 _____

25 _____

24 _____

23 _____

22 _____

21 _____

20 _____

19 _____

18 _____

17 _____

16 _____

15 _____

High School
and
Grade School

10 _____

0 _____

Delaying Gratification

Following a plan necessarily means delaying gratification. Turn to page 183 to review this concept. Admittedly, that's not always easy to do. It helps, though, if you are motivated and prepared. Answering the following questions should help you be both.

Turn to page 183 to review this concept.

Can you think of sacrifices you might need to make in order to achieve your goal? Might you need to give up some social activities, for example? Will you have to spend some of the money you now use for clothes or recreation for tuition? List them below.

_____

_____

_____

_____

What commitments are you *willing to make?* (Will you study for a certain amount of time every day? Will you take a job to earn money for school?)

_____

_____

_____

_____

List the rewards you hope to gain from those commitments and sacrifices below.

_____

_____

_____

Do the rewards make the sacrifices and commitments seem worthwhile?

_____

_____

Jodie's example: What do I want? *I want to be a lawyer.*

What are my choices right now? *To register for the advanced math class that will help me get into college and then law school, or to take the art class that would be more fun.*

I want to *be a lawyer,* **therefore, I will** *take the math class.*

What do I want? _____

What are my choices right now? _____

_____

_____

I want to _____ **, therefore, I will** _____ .

Facing Fears and Anxieties

In the space below, anticipate your fears by listing every excuse you can think of for giving up your dream.

_____

_____

_____

_____

Now list every reason or excuse you can think of for not successfully completing the preparation or training you need to have the career you want.

_____

_____

_____

YOUR PLAN FOR OVERCOMING FEARS

Now that you've faced your fears, take responsibility for them. For each excuse listed above, write an affirmation that counters the fear and gives you power. (See chapter 10.)

_____

_____

_____

_____

YOUR PLAN FOR OVERCOMING ROADBLOCKS
AND SOLVING PROBLEMS

Just as you are responsible for overcoming your own fears, you must take responsibility for solving your own problems. Can you think of any roadblocks or detours that might get in the way of your success during the next 10 years? (Review pages 203-215.) List those possibilities below.

1. _____

2. _____

3. _____

4. _____

Imagine your life 15 years from now. What will it be like if one of these events actually occurs?

_____

_____

_____

_____

Remember that you are in control of the situation. Can you think of things you can do now to avoid these problems? Write a goal and two objectives that will help you do that in the space below.

GOAL: _____

    Objective: _____

    _____

    Objective: _____

    _____

Your Action Plan for the Next 10 Years

Before you begin your detailed action plan for the next 10 years, sit down and visualize your life over this period of time. (See page 217 on visualizations.) How old will you be in 10 years? What do you think you'll look like? How do you want to feel about yourself and about your life? Once you have a clear picture of where you'd like to go and how you might get there, write your plans below. Word them as measurable objectives. (See pages 186 to 190 of *Career Choices*.)

My
10yearPlan
.com

Your 10-Year Goal _____

_____

279

YEAR ONE — (Next Year)   Your age _____

Education and training: _____

Living arrangements: _____

Employment: _____

Finances: _____

YEAR TWO

Education and training: _____

Living arrangements: _____

Employment: _____

Finances: _____

YEAR THREE

Education and training: _____

Living arrangements: _____

Employment: _____

Finances: _____

YEAR FOUR

Education and training: _____

Living arrangements: _____

Employment: _____

Finances: _____

YEAR FIVE

Education and training: _____

Living arrangements: _____

Employment: _____

Finances: _____

YEAR SIX

Education and training: _____

Living arrangements: _____

Employment: _____

Finances: _____

YEAR SEVEN

Education and training: _____

Living arrangements: _____

Employment: _____

Finances: _____

YEAR EIGHT

Education and training: _____

Living arrangements: _____

Employment: _____

Finances: _____

YEAR NINE

Education and training: _____

Living arrangements: _____

Employment: _____

Finances: _____

YEAR TEN

Education and training: _____

Living arrangements: _____

Employment: _____

Finances: _____

SUPPORTERS OF MY PLAN

Review page 262 on the importance of mentors. Can you think of people in your life right now who could be of assistance in reaching your goals? If so, list them below. If not, start watching for these important people to turn up in your life. Whether or not you know any now, you are sure to meet others in the next few years. Learn to recognize them, and be open to the things they have to teach you.

_____

_____

_____

MY MISSION IN LIFE

Back on page 61 you stated your mission in life. Is it still the same? Restate or rewrite it below and refer to it often. Although your mission may change, it will keep you on course. In the end, you are likely to judge your own success or failure according to how well you have lived up to this purpose.

_____

_____

_____

_____

Congratulations!

You have just completed a career and life planning process that will help you work toward the life YOU want. The outcome of this project is important to you, so you'll want to continue this process throughout your life.

Your life is defined by the choices you make.
— Mindy Bingham, author

The choices you make from this day forward will determine your life satisfaction.

The life-enhancing, decision-making process you've learned throughout your *Career Choices* coursework will help you along your journey to a self-sufficient adulthood.

Keep your 10-year plan current, updating your goals and objectives each year so you continue to envision and plan for a productive future. The skills you've just learned are ageless. Whether you are 14, 34, or 64 years old, they'll help walk you through the steps necessary for making the **best choices** for a life of personal fulfillment and happiness.

Remember, this step-by-step process can be used for all major decisions in your life. When you are faced with life-defining choices—where to live, who and when to marry, whether and when to have children, or which career you want and what level of education and training to pursue—you'll want to remember to ask yourself these three questions:

> Who Am I?
> What Do I Want?
> How Do I Get It?

Then pull out your *Career Choices Workbook and Portfolio* and, once again, work through these simple yet profound activities.

What you do with the plan you've developed will determine how happy you are and how successful you feel. With a productive vision of your future PLUS the energy to put your plans into action, you're bound to experience personal success.

My Career Portfolio Notebook

A career portfolio is a collection of the records, work samples, and certificates that demonstrates your qualifications, skills, experience, and achievements. You'll use your Career Portfolio notebook to exhibit your competencies to a potential employer or college recruiter. You'll also use it to track your accomplishments and plan for the training and skills you still need to acquire. The following format will allow you to easily update and customize your plans and record your accomplishments throughout life.

How to Assemble Your Career Portfolio Notebook

You need: A three-ring binder with a 2- or 3-inch spine
               A packet of 8 to 10 tabbed notebook dividers

Label the first tab Career Exploration Activities and the second tab Your Professional Development Plan. Make a photocopy of your completed *Career Choices* activities listed below and include them in the appropriate section of your Career Portfolio Notebook.

Section One—**Career Exploration Activities**

Activity	*Career Choices* Page	*Workbook/Portfolio* Page
Envisioning Your Future	14	6
Your Personal Profile bulls eye chart	27	11
Components of Lifestyle	63	28
Your Budget Profile for your desired lifestyle at age 29	92–93	42
Your Chart describing your ideal career characteristics	134	62
Career Interest Surveys	150–155	68–73
Career Decision-Making Chart	177	83

Section Two—**Your Professional Development Plan**

Activity	*Career Choices* Page	*Workbook/Portfolio* Page
Goal Setting Chart	189–190	87
Career Alternatives Ladder	246	109
Transferable Skills Chart	227	101
Job Application and Interview Questions	257–259	112–113
Your Education and Training 10-Year Plan	270–273	116–118
Your 10-Year Plan—Goals for education/training, living arrangements, employment and finances for the next 10 years	278–282	121–124

Update the charts and surveys listed above as you gain experience and change your goals and plans. Why not revise these each year around your birthday?

If your school allows you to keep your completed *Workbook and Portfolio*, slip it into the back cover pocket in your three-ring binder. If you change direction to follow a new dream, it will come in handy. You can always re-examine who you are, what you want, and how to get it by following the process you learned in *Career Choices* and reworking the activities in this workbook.

Section Three—**Interview Portfolio**

Now create a tab sheet for each of the bulleted topics listed below.

- Your resume
- Work or project samples
- Letters of recommendation
- Certificates, diplomas, awards
- Records of work experience (paid and unpaid)

This is the section that you'll take with you to interviews—whether with potential employers or college/trade school recruiters. Make it a habit to place these important documents in your three-ring binder as they are completed or acquired. That way, when an opportunity arises for an important interview, these essential records are readily available.

It will be rewarding to watch this section grow. For instance, whenever you receive a letter of recommendation (from a teacher, counselor, employer, or community source) you'll want to keep a copy in your portfolio. The same is true for copies of certificates, diplomas and awards. Employers and colleges like to see samples of your writing and technical skills so include written reports or photographs of completed projects. Your notebook will provide the date to easily revise your resume, work history or vita to include each new position, promotion or volunteer activity.

How and When to Use Your Career Portfolio

- **Career exploration and planning**—Be sure to take your portfolio notebook with you whenever you meet with your school counselors, mentors, teachers and career advisors. They will be better able to provide advice and personalized strategies if they can review your goals and plans, making your sessions together much more productive.

- **Employment and college/trade school interviews**—At the time of an interview, remove the documents in section three from your three-ring binder. You can give these documents a professional appearance by placing them in an appropriate jacket or presentation folder. You can find these presentation binders and portfolio covers at fine stationery stores or on the Internet.

- **Career changes**—Future workplace conditions or personal desires may dictate a career change, and your notebook will provide the framework for creating a new vision and plan for the future. Just follow the process you learned in this course.

Life is the sum of all your choices.
— Albert Camus

My10yearPlan.com®

My 10yearPlan.com provides an online planning area where you can enter the work from your *Career Choices Workbook and Portfolio*. This makes it easy to store, update, and share the data related to your 10-year plan. Depending on the level of access your school provides, you will enter the data from either the 25 activities essential for 10-year plan development or all of the nearly 100 *Career Choices* exercises using a dynamic and interactive format.

Once you input the information you've completed in your *Career Choices Workbook and Portfolio*, the My10yearPlan.com system uses it to create a **10-year Plan Summary Page**. This overview provides a snapshot of you and your dreams for the future, along with the goals and plans you've set for the next decade regarding your education and training, career, finances, and lifestyle choices.

How Do I Benefit from This Extra Step?

Because your 10-year plan is online, you can update it at any time while you are in high school.

As you learn and experience new things and your vision of your future continues to grow, all you have to do is go online and update your plan whenever you want.

You can easily share this plan with your advisors, counselors, teachers, parents, friends, and mentors.

The 10-year Plan Summary provides a snapshot of you—your dreams, goals, and plans. Anyone taking five minutes to read it will know a lot about you: who you are, what you want, and how you plan to go about getting it. Sessions with counselors will be more productive. Parents and friends can more effectively support your dreams and goals. Anyone reading your carefully-thought-out plan will be more likely to take you and your goals seriously.

Because it is online and easy to update, it provides a flexible tool as you change and grow.

The career you choose to create the first edition of your 10-year plan is meant for the duration of the course, not necessarily for the rest of your life. After all, they say most people will change careers five to seven times throughout their life. As you discover careers that hold even more interest, by going online and working through some of the key activities you'll be able to easily update your plan and keep it current.

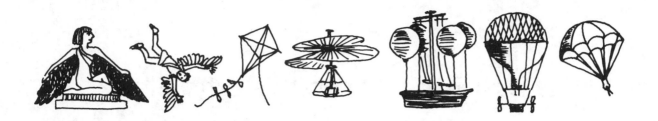

How to Use My10yearPlan.com and the Workbook Together

It's important to remember that your workbook and My10yearPlan.com are designed to work together in a two-step process.

1. After the classroom discussion that follows your reading of *Career Choices*, write your thoughts, ideas, and plans in your workbook.

2. Then, when you have access to the Internet, whether at home or at school, enter your data into your online 10-year plan.

Here are some important points to remember:

Always complete the activity in your workbook first.

Like most of your writing assignments, the work from your *Career Choices Workbook and Portfolio* will go through a number of different editorial stages. Think of your workbook as the place where you'll create your draft for each activity and think of My10yearPlan.com as the place for you to review, revise, edit, and polish your draft.

After you've completed the activity in your workbook, login to your My10yearPlan.com account and enter your information online.

This can happen whenever you have access to the Internet—whether it's during class time, after school in the library or career center, or at home during the evening.

Before you just start typing away, take a moment and read through the responses you've written in your workbook.

Maybe you've given the activity more thought since you first completed it. Do your answers still seem like the best possible response? If so, go ahead and enter the information into My10yearPlan.com as written. If not, you might want to update your answer as you type.

Keep in mind that the information you input into the activity pages of My10yearPlan.com will flow into your 10-year Plan Summary Page and your Portfolio Pages.

This is your chance to pay attention to your spelling, check for typos, and make sure you've answered in complete sentences when appropriate. Because you'll want to print and use your portfolio for job interviews, scholarship interviews, college interviews, and more, you'll want to make sure that your spelling, grammar, and punctuation are correct.

Finally, many teachers will use your Summary Page and your Portfolio Pages as part of your final grade.

Make sure you're always putting your best work into My10yearPlan.com so your grade reflects all of the thought and hard work you've devoted to this process.

Checkpoints

These checkpoints are simple statements that describe what you should expect to learn in each chapter. Known as learning objectives or learning outcomes, your task is to judge how well you understand each concept.

Once you finish a chapter, turn to the corresponding area of this checkpoint section and ask yourself, did I learn these concepts? Have I broadened my understanding about myself and the world around me?

If you feel confident in your understanding of the information, you'll want to move on to the next chapter. If you feel less confident, you need to flip back to that part of the chapter and work through it again, either on your own or with the help of your instructor, advisor, or learning partner.

Some people will read through these statements before they begin their work on each chapter to get a sense of what to expect. Others will wait until after they've experienced the material and then evaluate their comprehension. You'll need to determine the strategy that works best for you.

Who Am I?

Chapter 1

Envisioning Your Future: *How do you define success?*

You have started thinking about your ideal future, which is the first step toward achieving it. Before you move on, check to make sure that you've reached the goals listed below.

- ☐ I realized that success does not come from daydreaming, but from combining a vision with appropriate actions.
- ☐ I am beginning to imagine the kind of future that I would find most satisfying.
- ☐ I understand that work is more than just a way to earn a living; it is an important part of most people's identity.
- ☐ I can now recognize the diversity in individual's daily accomplishments.
- ☐ I am aware of the methods that I typically use to make decisions and can evaluate their effectiveness.
- ☐ I learned there are myriad definitions of success, and I realize the one I want to strive to meet is my own.
- ☐ I am now on a life-long path toward determining my own personal definition of success.

Chapter 2

Your Personal Profile: *Getting what you want starts with knowing who you are*

You have now made good progress toward answering the question "Who am I?" which you will continue to investigate throughout your life. You also recognize that knowing yourself well is essential to living the most fulfilling life possible. Make sure you are ready to proceed by confirming that you've accomplished the goals below.

- ☐ I am starting to outline the many qualities and characteristics that make up my unique identity and understand this self-knowledge is a necessary and ongoing part of any rewarding life.

- ☐ I am learning to identify and articulate things that are extremely important to me on an emotional level.

- ☐ I clarified which work values are most meaningful in my own life.

- ☐ I determined my work behavioral style and understand it as an important trait to consider when evaluating my career interests.

- ☐ I identified the strengths that make me unique and valuable, and I am starting to synthesize how my interests, values, and traits relate to education and career choices.

- ☐ I understand the standard skills categories, and I'm cataloging the skills I've developed over the years.

- ☐ I recognized and evaluated my roles, occupations, and vocations.

- ☐ I am more aware of the messages—verbal and otherwise—I get from society and from significant people in my life, and I understand how these messages can affect the way I feel about my future or my potential.

- ☐ I completed the first draft of my bulls-eye formatted personal profile, with the recognition that I will build on this as I discover more about myself.

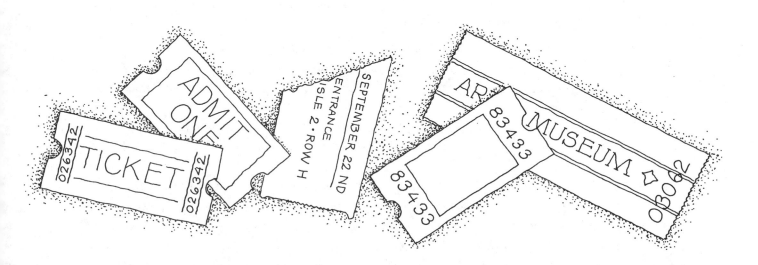

What Do I Want?

Chapter 3
Lifestyles of the Satisfied and Happy: *Keeping your balance and perspective*

You have begun to answer the question "What do I want?" as it relates to your ideal lifestyle. Check that you've reached the goals listed below, essential for living a balanced and satisfying life.

- ☐ I understand Maslow's hierarchy of needs and its impact on my identity and self-esteem.
- ☐ I started to identify an overall goal or mission for my life.
- ☐ I projected myself into the future and recognized the diversity of lifestyle options available to me.
- ☐ I identified the components of a balanced lifestyle and appreciate the desirability of balancing internal and external, personal and professional, private and public life.
- ☐ I experienced the balanced lifestyle evaluation process and realized the effect that outside forces can have on my life and my role in mitigating these.

Chapter 4
What Cost this Lifestyle? *Every career choices involves sacrifices and rewards*

You now have a strong understanding of the costs of any given lifestyle—financial costs, psychological costs, and the costs in terms of commitment to a given career. This knowledge will likely impact your career selection, so take the time to make sure you've mastered the concepts below.

- ☐ I completed a comprehensive budget for the lifestyle I aspire to once I complete my education/training.
- ☐ I realize just how many financial obligations I have to consider in my budget and understand the effect career choice will have on my lifestyle.
- ☐ I experienced the most common budgeting technique—taking a given income and deciding how it should be allocated.
- ☐ I discussed some causes of poverty and understand ways in which I might best avoid becoming a poverty statistic myself.
- ☐ I explored the myth that money will make me happy.
- ☐ I learned that there are sacrifices as well as rewards associated with every job and every lifestyle. I can now evaluate any career I am considering more objectively and determine whether or not that career would be a wise choice for me.
- ☐ I recognize the rewards and sacrifices of specific careers as they relate to my work values and realize that values not satisfied on the job can be met with appropriate after-hours activities.
- ☐ I recognize the long-term financial payoff of an investment in further education.
- ☐ I interviewed friends and acquaintances and gained specific information about the costs and rewards of various jobs.
- ☐ I realize that to meet long-term goals I will have to make short-term sacrifices, and I explored a systematic decision-making rubric that can help me attain my goals.

Chapter 5
Your Ideal Career: *There's more to consider than just the work*

You have now taken a look at the general characteristics you hope to find in a job. This will eventually help you to identify your ideal career. Before moving forward, confirm that you've achieved each of the goals below.

- ☐ I completed a series of questionnaires and identified the specific working conditions and job characteristics that most appeal to me.
- ☐ I considered the job characteristics that are most important to me, and I'm thinking creatively about jobs that meet those requirements.
- ☐ I analyzed which skills I'd most like to use in my ideal job.
- ☐ I considered a variety of formats for structured or unstructured employment and gauged my level of anxiety tolerance in relation to working.
- ☐ I evaluated whether my attitudes, characteristics, and skills are more in line with the role of employer or of employee.
- ☐ I started to sort out my feelings about status as it relates to job selection.

Chapter 6
Career Research: *Reading about careers isn't enough*

You have now explored a valuable three-step process for learning about and deciding on a career. You have started to narrow down career choices that might suit you best. Before you make that decision in the next chapter, confirm each of the following statements.

- ☐ I understand the 16 career clusters and the types of jobs in each.
- ☐ I reviewed and considered my personality traits, financial requirements, ideal working conditions, and projected lifestyle as I begin narrowing down my optimal careers.
- ☐ I learned library and online research skills and put them to use in evaluating information about potential careers.
- ☐ I completed at least three Career Interest Surveys for careers that appeal to me.
- ☐ I visualized what it would be like to spend a typical day at the job of my choice.
- ☐ I practiced writing a business letter and conducting an interview.
- ☐ I saw first-hand what it might be like to spend a day at my chosen career either through job shadowing or volunteering.
- ☐ I can identify jobs within an industry that match my work behavioral style.
- ☐ I identified a specific job I consider a good match for my personality and work behavioral style.

Chapter 7
Decision-making: *How to choose what's best for you*

Congratulations! You have arrived at a preliminary career decision that you will use as you develop your 10-year plan. Just as importantly, you understand that this career decision can be changed as you continue to learn more about yourself and the world around you. Before you start exploring how to obtain your chosen career, make sure you've mastered the following tasks.

☐ I clarified the difference between long- and short-term goals, and I recognize the importance of considering my plans for the future when making daily decisions.

☐ I understand that before evaluating different options I need to identify factors surrounding each option and, with those facts in mind, determine the probable outcomes of each option.

☐ I learned how to evaluate the pros, cons, and likelihood of success of different choices.

☐ I completed a systematic decision-making rubric to determine the career that most closely matches my goals and needs.

☐ I understand that my own resources, wants, and needs should be factored when making major life decisions, and I know how I can use the decision-making rubric for those choices.

☐ I evaluated the strengths and weaknesses of my decision-making strategies.

How Do I Get It?

Chapter 8
Setting Goals and Solving Problems: *Skills for successful living*

You have made great progress in making the plans, learning the skills, and acquiring the tools you will need to realize your dreams. Solving problems and setting goals are two of the most important skills for developing any action plan. Check out the objectives below to ensure that you've met them.

☐ I learned how to apply problem-solving techniques that involve delaying gratification, accepting responsibility, and striking a balance between pleasure and discipline.

☐ I learned the process for writing quantitative goals and objectives.

☐ I learned to write quantitative goals and objectives of my own including those that relate to my lifestyle goals.

☐ I understand the cycle of growth and I'm aware of opportunities to expand my goals as I develop new values and ideas for my future.

Chapter 9
Avoiding Detours and Roadblocks:
The road to success is dotted with many tempting parking places

We all know that problems and challenges are a fact of life. You have learned strategies that will help you face them head-on to actively overcome them. Since you are responsible for your own life, you recognize that it is up to you to overcome any perceived limitations. These are powerful lessons, so confirm that you've completed the following objectives before moving on.

☐ I examined common excuses people use for not doing what they can or want to do. I evaluated those reasons and determined what might be done to avoid using them myself.

☐ I started to evaluate my own excuses and look at them in a new way. By accepting responsibility for my problems, I am also opening new avenues for solving them.

☐ After reviewing some unsettling statistics regarding poverty, earnings, and retirement, I better understand how I can address these in my own life.

☐ I examined some common problems and, by projecting into the future, I considered possible long-term consequences of present actions.

☐ I personalized the effect of dropping out of school on my eventual job satisfaction.

☐ I comprehend the financial costs of bad habits, both current and long term.

☐ I understand how flexibility and salary impact the ability to mix career and family, and recognize that women would do well to consider careers not traditionally pursued by females.

☐ I learned evaluation techniques that I can use before impulsively abandoning a dream or plan.

☐ I am learning to overcome fears I may have by simply imagining myself as successful at that which makes me anxious.

☐ I learned a hierarchical approach to conquering anxieties that might limit my future goals.

☐ I started the process of a 10-year plan by making long-range plans for someone who could reasonably be expected to fail due to lack of resources.

☐ I observed that taking calculated risks is an important skill.

Chapter 10
Attitude is Everything: *Learning to accentuate the positive*

You have begun to develop the attitudes that will lead you to your own definition of success. It may take practice to fully integrate these new attitudes, but you will find that the payoff is well worth it. Check below to make sure you'll have all the tools needed.

- ☐ I understand the power of affirmation in changing self-limiting attitudes.
- ☐ I wrote my own affirmations to keep me on track to meet my goals.
- ☐ I recognize the characteristics and attitudes of excellence.
- ☐ I realize that aggressive action may be necessary to achieve some goals.
- ☐ I clarified the concept of the work ethic and can recognize it in others as well as in myself.
- ☐ I strategized ways to improve work habits to insure job security and promotion.
- ☐ I recognize the attitudes most in demand for workers—now and in the future.
- ☐ I developed an action plan to change any self-limiting attitudes.
- ☐ I identified the attitudes and skills needed to compete in this ever-changing world of the 21st century.
- ☐ I recognize the dignity in all work.

Chapter 11
Getting Experience: *Finding your first job*

You have now been introduced to some of the most basic job hunting skills—writing resumes, locating jobs, filling out job applications, and succeeding in informational and job interviews. If you haven't already, you'll certainly want to consult other resources for more in-depth information and tools, particularly those found online.   Check that you've learned these basics concepts listed below.

- ☐ I wrote my own resume.
- ☐ I know how to conduct an informational interview.
- ☐ I am familiar with the dos and don'ts of job interviews as well as some questions that I can expect to be asked.
- ☐ I practiced filling out a job application.
- ☐ I gained insight on dealing with rejection and accepting a job.

Chapter 12
Where Do You Go from Here? *Writing your 10-year plan*

You now should have the resources you need to move forward. You have gathered the information and developed the skills to write a comprehensive and meaningful 10-year plan that is personalized to your own unique goals, personality, and mission in life. You have also learned decision-making techniques that will continue to help you throughout your life as you encounter change. Make sure you've covered all of the following topics, and you'll be on your way!

- ☐ I conducted a final review of my Career Interest Surveys and decision-making rubrics to determine the career that most closely matches me and my plans for the future.

- ☐ I conducted online research and understand the various education and job training opportunities that are available to me, particularly for my chosen career field.

- ☐ I not only developed an Education and Training 10-Year Plan, but I also understand that life-long learning is necessary in the 21st century.

- ☐ I recognize the importance of delaying gratification by identifying the sacrifices and commitments required to achieve the greatest reward.

- ☐ I wrote affirmations to empower me as I overcome fears that might hold me back from achieving my dream.

- ☐ I identified things I can do now to avoid roadblocks I'm likely to encounter.

- ☐ I defined my 10-year goal and wrote my 10-year plan to get there, taking education, living arrangements, employment, and finances into account.

- ☐ I acknowledge my responsibility to ask for help when I need it and I know how to recognize potential mentors when I meet them.

- ☐ I refined my own personal definition of success.

- ☐ I confirmed or refined my own personal mission statement and understand the role it plays in guiding me through future choices and changes.

Homework Assignments and Grades

_____

_____

_____

_____

_____

_____

_____

_____

_____

_____

_____

_____

_____

_____

_____

_____